D1035944

Michael's Christmas Card

Michael's Christmas Card

A Life's Journey Through

the Prism of Christmas

Michael Bossone

WISDOM/WORK
Published by Wisdom/Work
Wilmington, North Carolina

Published 2022

Copyright © 2022 by Michael Bossone

ISBN 978-1-7377227-5-5

Printed in the United States of America

Set in Adobe Garamond Pro
Designed by Abigail Chiaramonte

All rights reserved. No part of this book may be reproduced in any
form on by an electronic or mechanical means, including information storage and retrieval systems, without permission in writing
from the publisher, except by a reviewer who may quote brief
passages in a review.

This book is dedicated to my wife, Tressy.
She is my all. She is my every. She is my only.

Introduction

SOMETHING IMPORTANT TO SAY

Twelve hours ago, I was lying on the mosaic tile floor of the Sistine Chapel staring up at Michelangelo's paintings on the ceiling, humbly thanking God for the countless blessings in my life that have allowed such a miraculous moment to take place. I have gazed up at these masterpieces many times, but in this moment it was clear that my perspective allowed me to see it all with new vision. Though I was alone, through the product of divinely-inspired human creative genius, I could feel the enormity of the Universe embracing me. For my entire life I have been seeking... seeking love... seeking beauty... seeking truth... seeking God... and there, with the cold marble below me and the colors of heaven above me, I found much more than I was seeking.

Twenty-nine years ago, I was sitting in my four-teenth-floor Greenwich Village apartment staring out the window at the World Trade Center, desperately seeking a respite from my law school studies. It was exam time, the most stressful and isolating time of law school (which is itself a stressful and isolating time), and I was finding it difficult to focus on my Evidence outline. So with my next exam less than twenty-four hours away, I left my books behind and decided to go for a walk, seeking inspiration from the streets of the city and the brisk December air. I found much more than I was seeking.

One block behind my apartment building was (but unfortunately no longer still is) a lovely retail store owned by a young French couple. They specialized in posters, CDs, and greeting cards, all imported from France. I particularly enjoyed the ambiance of the place, and often purchased cards there for friends and loved ones. In the madness of our reading period and the end of the semester, a few weeks had passed since my last visit, and I was delighted to find that a selection of Christmas cards had been added to the usual offerings.

Other than to my immediate family and past girl-friends, I had never given Christmas cards to anyone. I recalled my mother's annual trip to Main Pharmacy in downtown Manasquan, New Jersey, her carefully select-ing the right card from the large books full of samples, the list of recipients from the previous year, the scribbles in the address book, and the licking of the envelopes and stamps. It had never occurred to me that I should now be partaking in this ritual. The sending of Christmas cards was for adults…for people with more life experience…for those who had something important to say.

I found an image and inscription that felt right, handed the young French woman my credit card, and returned to my apartment. Instead of turning to my exam preparation, I put pen to paper and drafted a paragraph-long sentiment that I wanted to share with those who meant the most to me. Perhaps for the first time, I believed I had something important to say to them, something about the true meaning of Christmas and the role that I believed God, family, and friends should play in our lives. In a world that was becoming increasingly more complicated, these words provided both a catharsis for me and a little piece of myself to those I love.

In that moment, I vowed to myself that I was going to create a new Christmas tradition. That from here on out, for the rest of my life, no matter how busy or chaotic my life was, I was going to share my perspective with the people who mean the most to me, and I was going to do it through the written word.

That was December 1993. I was 24 years old.

It's now 2022, and at 53 years old, I can say that I have kept my vow. Each and every December for the past two and three-quarter decades, I have created a small window of serenity in a life that has been anything but serene. And within that window I have claimed my own piece of reflective space, and documented the state of my heart, mind, and soul at that specific time of my life.

Each December I printed my reflections, folded each piece of paper twice, and placed them inside my

Christmas card. Each year my Christmas card list grew, as did the connections between my loved ones and me. It meant something to me that my words meant something to them.

It was many years after I began that both my wife and my mother encouraged me to gather them together to tell a complete story, and the result is the book that you hold in your hands.

What follows is the story of my life… a story that has been written one chapter per year over 28 years. I have resisted the strong urge to edit what and how I wrote so many years ago, for we are who we were. And as I read some of my earliest reflections, I recognize and remember the voice of that young man. And I hope that young man would be proud of the person I am today.

It is my genuine hope that in sharing with you my development as a writer and a person, you will come to appreciate your own development over the years.

I now understand, not only that I have something important to say, but that we all have something important to say. I pray that you find the courage to tell your story, that you are heard by the people who love you, and that you hear the story of those you love.

1993

24 years old

May the sacred Spirit of Christmas provide the fullness
and contentment that we all seek in our everyday lives.

May we all strive to reach our potential
and to treat each other
all year long with the warm hearts and gentle smiles
that come so easily at Christmas time.

The Spirit of Christmas is alive:
in our spouses, in our children, and in our friends;
in our sacred basilicas and in our humble homes;
it is a vibrant life-force that manifests itself in our
confidence in ourselves, in our respect for others, and in
the dignity and decency with which we live our lives.

It is not just a one-month feeling: it is now, it is forever,
it is eternal. The Spirit of Christmas is alive in us all.

1994

25 years old

May a child play in your spirit,
May love motivate your will,
May you be at peace with your thoughts,
May you be proud of your actions,
May God be in your heart,
and may angels kiss your soul.

1995

26 years old

Over my twenty-six years, Christmas has come to mean many things to me. There was a time when Christmas was the presents stacked under and around our tree. Once Christmas was a jolly ol' chap with snowy white whiskers and a sprite lit'l reindeer with a shiny red nose. Christmas was a week or two off from school and endless trips to the mall. Christmas was glowing lights and glossy red balls, garland and tinsel, The Grinch on tv, and running out of scotch tape.

Then Christmas was more. It was a traditional Italian Christmas Eve feast of fish, fish and more fish: a symbolic celebration of familial love and affection that bonds generation to generation. It was a breaking of bread and drinking of wine with those who mean the most to me. Christmas was my grandmother in the kitchen and another new niece or nephew at the table. Christmas was a toast from my father, a hug from my mother, and a magical, musical midnight moment as baby Jesus is placed in the manger. Christmas was that house on the hill at 713 Howell Drive and the smiles on the faces of those within.

Well, this year my Christmas will be spent with Tressy's family in Atlanta. Sure, Christmas will be an extended phone call back to the house on the hill, but it will also be the opportunity to grow ever closer to my new family. The house will be different and the food will be different and the noise level will certainly be different, but the love and compassion and appreciation will be the same. Christmas will be Polish French toast and kielbasa on Christmas morning, midnight mass at Sacred Heart, my topping the tree with the angel, and most importantly, a midnight embrace from the love of my life.

Before I know it, Tressy and I will be creating Christmas traditions of our own and the circle will start anew. Through our children, Christmas will once again be presents stacked under and around the tree, glowing lights and a reindeer with a shiny red nose. And then the meaning of Christmas will begin to transform for our children as it has for me.

Through the years Christmas has come to mean so many different things, its meaning has changed so greatly, that I still repeatedly ask myself what Christmas is fundamentally all about?

It is this question that always leads me back to the Word. I guess it's not Christmas that has changed over the years, but rather it is I who have changed, and am still changing. Christmas still means what it has always and will always mean: Christmas is joy, the unparalleled and eternal happiness in our hearts and souls that springs from that divine child born on the holiest of nights.

May you and your family experience the joy of Christmas in your heart, mind and spirit, and may we all reach out to extend love, compassion, and kindness to those less fortunate than ourselves.

1996

27 years old

Christmas is a time of creation. It is a moment of transition from the fire and brimstone of the Old Testament to the love and peace of the New; from the despair of a world in need of a savior to the joy of that savior's birth; from darkness to light; from potentiality to actuality; from ethereality to flesh; from cacophonous clatter to melodious music.

Christmas is a time of creation. It is a season of transition from the mayhem and madness of our everyday existence to the kindness and serenity of the Christmas spirit. Perhaps this change is no more evident than in the joyous sounds of the holidays. Instead of our usual audible fare - the background noise of a television, the FM pop blaring out from the car beside us, the idle chatter of useless arguments - we are treated to the beauty of the Music of Christmas. From the playfulness of 'Jingle Bells' to the majesty of 'O Holy Night,' we are touched

- we are affected - in a way that only art can touch us. Through the music of Christmas, we gain insight into the world around us and our place in that world. Through the music of Christmas, we grow in our love for our friends, our family, our God, and ourselves. Through the music of Christmas, we are connected.

This year was a time of creation for Tressy and me, as we committed ourselves to each other and created a union of love and friendship. Not surprisingly, music played a pivotal role in our wedding celebration at Notre Dame, from the lone violin playing 'Canon in D' during our Wedding Mass in the Basilica to Springsteen's 'Twist & Shout' that ended our day-and-nightlong reception with a bang. Hearing those songs now stirs up memories of that special day and brings us right back to those moments.

The music of Christmas has that same power. These songs transport us back in time to the beauty and warmth of Christmases past, while at the same time helping us forge new memories for the future.

This Christmas, as we prepare for our holiday visit to the East Coast, while packing our wrapped presents in our suitcases and searching for what few winter clothes we have left after moving to Arizona, we wish you a holiday season filled with the music of laughter, the music of reconciliation and good will, and the music of faith and hope... and wish that all of your holiday hopes are realized and all of your Christmas dreams come true.

1997

28 years old

Every beautiful event in life is preceded by the equally beautiful anticipation of that event. Christmas is no exception. Every year, for the first few weeks of December, our hearts and minds look forward to the miracle of Christmas. And at some point, after all the presents are under the tree and all of the cookies are baked, we all come to that moment when the anticipation of the miracle ends and the miracle itself begins, when Christmas potentiality is transformed into Christmas actuality, and the most joyous celebration of Christ's birth begins.

Back at my parents' home in New Jersey, that moment when Christmas actually begins has always been an easy one to identify. It would be around 5pm on Christmas Eve, when the rest of my family was still working down at the Squan Tavern, partly to take care of the last few customers in for dinner, and partly to continue preparing for the Christmas Eve feast that would begin about 9pm.

I would always be at home alone, finishing setting the table, choosing the music for the evening and making sure everything would be perfect for all of our guests.

About that time the doorbell would ring for the first of many, many times that night. It was always that moment, the arrival of our first guest, that began Christmas for me, and it was always my Aunt Anita on the other side of the front door. Year after year, she arrived at that door with two things: the world's greatest cream-puffs, and more importantly, her unforgettably gentle smile. It would be at least another hour or two until any other guests would arrive, and the two of us always spent that time in the den just talking. I looked forward to that time with her every year. It felt warm...it felt comfortable...it felt like Christmas.

This Christmas, Tressy and I will be celebrating the holidays in Atlanta. And though it's still an adjustment to be away from 713 Howell Drive on Christmas Eve, this year I'm somewhat thankful that I'll be somewhere else. Because if I were there, I would be sitting around waiting for the doorbell to ring around 5pm, and of course, it wouldn't. I guess God needed another soprano in His choir of angels, and Aunt Anita will be celebrating Christmas with Him from now on.

And even in Atlanta, as 5pm approaches, I'll be thinking of her, and her creampuffs, and her gentle smile, and I'll wonder how Christmas will know how to make that leap from potential to actual without that doorbell ever ringing. But you know, something tells me that when that time comes, I'll close my eyes, and shed a tear or two, and in my mind I'll hear that doorbell ring...and this year, and forever more, Aunt Anita will still be right there with me...and Christmas will begin.

May Christmas begin in your heart and remind you of what is important ...may you remember loved ones who have moved on ...and may the joy and peace of Christmas help you approach each day with an appreciation for those around you who make life such a beautiful gift.

1998

29 years old

The Gift

On Christmas Eve at a house in Brielle, New Jersey, and on Christmas Morning at a house in Morrow, Georgia, many gifts will be received. Only one will really matter.

This gift will not be found in a box, wrapped in shiny paper, topped with a bow and placed beneath a Christmas tree. It cannot be purchased in a store, through a catalogue or over the internet. It will come from as far away as heaven and from as near as our own hearts. And it will stay with us forever.

Helen Barbara Olejniczak Pawlik was born outside Warsaw, Poland in 1907. Two years earlier, Yolanda Cecero Bossone was born in the small town of Casapulla, Italy. For the past ninety or so years, these two extraordinary women lived their lives according to principles and ideologies that are as foreign to many present-day

Americans as America itself was to them when they first crossed the Atlantic. Through two world wars, through the development of radio, film, television, telephones, computers, airplanes and space travel, through economic depressions and personal tragedies, each put her trust in God and raised a family. Through years of adversity and challenges unknowable to our generation, they worked to breathe life into those families, to infuse them with the traditional culture of the Old World, and to educate them with the integrity necessary to succeed in the New.

As the years passed, their families blossomed under their loving guidance. They became grandmothers, and great grandmothers, and each proudly took her place as the matriarch of her little piece of the world.

Three months ago, under her own terms, Helen closed her eyes and turned her soul skyward. One day soon, Yolanda will do the same.

This Christmas, and every Christmas, the families who will gather in those two houses will continue to receive a very special gift. Every man, woman, and child will receive the legacy of familial love and a tradition of compassion from the courageous women whose inner-strength, faith, and fortitude made us what we are today.

With that gift comes the responsibility and obligation to continue that tradition with future generations and to honor that legacy that we are so blessed to receive. Keeping their legacy alive is our gift to them.

This Christmas, may every member of the Pawlik and Bossone families find Helen's and Yolanda's love in our hearts, helping us to move beyond petty differences and appreciate the gift that binds us together. And may all of our friends take a moment to honor the legacy of the ones who came before, the ones who taught us all what it means to love and be loved.

1999

30 years old

THE CHRISTMAS TRAIN

Sometimes one finds Christmas in the strangest of places. This year, I found it on July 24th in section 2 of the Continental Airlines Arena in East Rutherford, New Jersey.

My artistic idol, Bruce Springsteen, was finishing up the 4th of 15 sold-out shows at the Meadowlands. Tressy and I had flown in from Scottsdale to see our first of many shows from this tour, Bruce's first with the E-Street Band in 10 years. He ended that magical show with a song he had written just a few months earlier to celebrate the re-birth of his band, and this was the first time I had heard "Land of Hope and Dreams." It has echoed in my mind ever since.

Inspiration for this song came partly from African American spirituals like "This Train Is Bound For Glory" which promises a triumphant ride out of oppression and adversity for the righteous and the holy. For decades that song has inspired faith in those yearning for re-birth. But where it requires its passengers to live lives free of sin, Bruce welcomes all of us sinners onto his train with the understanding that all of those sins will be forgiven if our hearts are true. On July 24th I boarded that train… a train of hope, a train of redemption, but most of all, a train of faith.

What moved me most about Bruce's new song was a very simple but incredibly powerful line: "Faith will be rewarded." I remember the words leaping out of his mouth and into my soul, as he and I both stood with our right hands raised high in the air, open-palmed in reverence of a higher power. Three months later we stood in those same positions, this time in Los Angeles, and this time with tears welling up in my eyes.

I had recently been told that my mother had been diagnosed with breast cancer. Thank God they caught it early, but the initial shock and horror of waiting for those phone calls each day and not being able to be right there beside her were almost unbearable. I was spending a great deal of my time praying, and I found myself repeatedly returning to Bruce's lyrics in that song: "Tomorrow there'll be sunshine and all this darkness past," "Dreams will not be thwarted," and most of all, "Faith will be rewarded."

And it made me take a closer look at faith. Faith is divinely-inspired potentiality; it is intrinsically forward-looking. For once a hope or dream is realized, it becomes fact. It becomes history. It becomes experience. But before that hope or dream is realized, it is held in one's heart and it is kept alive by one's faith. Faith is the confidence we have in ourselves, in each other, and in our God that we will one day reach that land of our hopes and our dreams.

God welcomes everyone, saints and sinners, losers and winners, on the train to His kingdom. And it is in His grace that we find the greatest faith of all: the faith that God had in us to believe we were worthy of receiving his only Son. From His holy faith comes a star, a manger, and a young couple. From His holy faith comes the birth of a glorious child. From His holy faith comes Christmas.

So to all our friends and family...

when we live our days trying to do what is right rather than what is easy, remember ... faith will be rewarded.

when we disregard petty disagreements, and choose instead to love one another as we are, remember ... faith will be rewarded.

when we realize the baby in the manger means more than the presents under the tree, remember ... faith will be rewarded.

And to my mother...

when you see me by your side in floral rainbows and popsicle stick picture frames, remember ... faith will be rewarded.

2000

31 years old

HER CHRISTMAS TOUCH

I already received my Christmas gifts this year...long before December 25th. My mother courageously fought and won her battle with breast cancer, and then began her quest to help others in their fight. My in-laws selflessly agreed to spend their first Christmas away from home in twenty years so we could experience our traditional Christmas Eve together as an extended family. And Tressy brought into this world the greatest gift any man could ever receive: a beautiful and healthy child. But my father got the jump on all of them. Back in February he granted me a special gift at one of the most difficult times in his life.

Tressy and I had just recently discovered that we were pregnant. We were so overjoyed by our own news that we were caught unprepared when we received the phone call from New Jersey. My grandmother, Yolanda Cecere Bossone, the matriarch of our family and my spiritual and moral compass, had taken a grave turn for the worse. After ninety-four years of living one of the greatest lives I have been blessed to encounter, it was clear that her time left with us would be brief. Although we had said our final goodbyes to each other long before, my heart still felt unsettled. There was one more thing I needed her to know.

For years I had been dreaming of the day when I would have a child of my own. I had played out the circumstances of my child's birth in my head thousands of times. Like the rest of my brothers and sisters, I would drive with my child straight from the hospital to our restaurant and would park right by the back door. I would carry my child to the door, and there we would be met by Gram. In a ritual that blended the realms of faith, love, and superstition, Gram would hold that new baby in her arms, and the most miraculous moment would occur. Being held in Gram's arms, that child would be baptized into our family. My child, through Gram's touch, would inherit the full power of our traditions and familial love. It was perhaps the moment I most looked forward to in my life, when my past would become one with my future. It would be the defining moment when life would be transformed... from ordinary to extraordinary...from common to sacred.

As I talked on the phone to my father, with Gram slowly slipping away just a few feet away from him in a hospital bed, the weight of a weary world came crashing down upon me as I came to the realization that Gram would never hold my child; that the image of her holding my flesh and blood in her hands would never exist anywhere but in my quickly dying dreams. So fighting back tears, I asked my father to tell Gram the only thing in my heart that I never had the chance to share with her; something my father and our families did not yet know. I knew the time was now or never, so through sobs I spoke the words to my father, and my father whispered the words in Gram's ear, "Tressy's pregnant. Michael and Tressy are going to have a baby." She was in and out of consciousness that day, but I know she heard my father's words, and I know she understood them. Gram fell asleep that night…for the last time.

As I sit here now looking into the dark eyes of my two-month-old son, I wonder if perhaps the moment that I dreamed about my whole life is still possible. It might take a miracle, but isn't that what Christmas is all about?

On December 21st Tressy and I will travel back to New Jersey for Christmas and introduce Aidan to the fruit of my grandmother's labor. We will bring him to my parents' restaurant that was born thirty-six years ago from her cooking. On Christmas Eve we will gather at my parents' house for the traditional Christmas Eve feast which Gram carried with her from the old world to the new. The house will be filled with the aromas of Gram's recipes as my brother continues her legacy in the kitchen.

And at the end of the table set for forty people, there will be an empty chair. There amongst her great grandchildren, at the kids' table where she most enjoyed sitting, we will set a place for her to honor her memory. And at some point during that night, when no one is looking, I will sit in that chair with Aidan in my arms, and we'll close our eyes, and we'll both feel Gram's arms around us, and life will be transformed...from ordinary to extraordinary...from common to sacred.

2001

32 years old

O Come All Ye Faithful

Preparing for Christmas is never easy. Every year it seems to take us more time, more energy, and more money to get ready for the celebration of this special day. But this year, in addition to our long list of Christmas errands, we have harsh realities to face. The attacks of September 11th and their aftermath have hit us hard in a place that always seemed so well protected. They broke through that which seemed unbreakable. They made us question that which we had always assumed.

So the questions may be asked, will Christmas somehow feel different this year? With so much sadness, fear, and anger in the world, are all of us ready to celebrate Christmas?

I recently found my answer in the first line of an old Christmas carol, in the journey of a three-inch-long piece of painted ceramic, and in the eyes of my fourteen-month-old little boy.

Every Christmas Eve my entire family gathers at my parents' home in New Jersey for our traditional Italian celebration. Many of the traditions of that night are very old and have been passed down through hundreds of years and across continents. The tradition I most look forward to is the placing of baby Jesus in the manger at midnight. Many years ago my father created a wonderful ceremony around this moment. Our entire family gathers around the manger, and while my father plays a sacred Christmas hymn, he hands the little ceramic baby Jesus to his youngest grandchild. When that child places baby Jesus in the manger, Christmas Eve ends and Christmas begins.

A few months ago, amidst all of the madness, terror, and travel nightmares, Tressy and I decided that we would spend Christmas in Arizona this year. But I asked my father if he would allow me to choose the music to accompany the manger ceremony, so that in some way I could still participate in that magical moment. He agreed. One recent Saturday morning, Aidan and I got out all of our Christmas CDs in search of a song that would be appropriate for the unique circumstances of this year.

The first words of the very first song we played struck me silent: "O come all ye faithful, joyful and triumphant." As I stood listening to this song, adoring and embracing my little boy as he looked into my eyes, I heard a very timely message in those opening words. These words are a calling, a passionate request for us to come together for a very special purpose at a very special time. And this is not an open invitation; rather, it is directed solely to we people of faith, to we people who believe even when reason and logic give us reason to doubt.

On that starry night in Bethlehem, similar to now, there was danger and fear in the world. Shepherds and kings came then; we are called to come now. We people of faith are being called together to celebrate the birth of a child: a child whose destiny is to give us the strength to rise above our fears, to give us the compassion to forgive those who do us harm. This is our time to unite in love and peace. This is our time to answer the call, to arrive full of joy and triumph, ready to adore and embrace the child who will take those fears away. This is Christmas.

And so I come to Christmas this year...

with my wife at my side and my son in my arms...

joyous and triumphant...

with faith in my heart...

prepared to celebrate, not just the wondrous birth of that child, but all that is very, very right with the world.

2002

33 years old

Aidan's Favorite Action Figure

Yesterday, ten days before Christmas, I sat down to read the Sunday paper. As I was settling into my favorite paper-reading chair, the hundreds of inserts that are stuffed into the paper every week proved to be too heavy, and the myriad, colorful flyers fell across the floor. As I gathered up the garish advertising booklets, I found myself paying particular attention to the circular from Toys 'R' Us. They were advertising their best prices of the Christmas season, and the pages were decorated with bells and wreaths and other nondescript symbols of holiday cheer.

The entire front page of this magazine-thick ad was devoted to action figures, many of which are some of the hottest toys for 2002. There I saw Sharon Osbourne, Harry Potter and his Slime Chamber, and Pokemon

Venusaur with his Razor Leaf. And for just around ten dollars more, I could purchase an extra-large version of either the Masters of the Universe Evil Enemy, Skeletor, or Spawn's Jackal Assassin. And sure, buried back on page nine I located the adorable Fisher Price Little People characters, of whom Aidan is particularly fond. But for the most part, these action figures, with their spikes and skulls and potions and sputtering British husbands, were being peddled as appropriate gifts for the celebration of Christ's birth.

And right then it hit me, like a snowball in the face, that my "celebrate the true meaning of Christmas" ideology that I have carefully crafted throughout my adult years is about to be challenged as never before. Aidan is now twenty-six months old, but before I know it he will be six, and he will be going to school with children who will ask for (and undoubtedly receive) such things for Christmas, and they will bring them to school for show-and-tell, and when asked by their teacher how their Christmas was they will say things like, "Great, I got Skeletor… and a PlayStation2… and a new bike and…" And it is my job, somehow, to do and say the hundreds of things that need to be done and said each and every day, so that my little boy can look at his teacher and his friends when someone asks that same question and answer without mentioning a single toy or gift.

Call me naïve. Call me overly idealistic. Call me a dinosaur advocating an ethic that has been lost and/or forgotten. But when I look into expressive eyes of my two-year-old little boy, how can I treat my responsibility to do and say those hundreds of things each day with anything but the utmost seriousness and respect?

Yes, we will be buying Aidan Christmas presents (though never as many as I received as a child), and I am greatly looking forward to his sneaking down the steps when he thinks Tressy and I are still asleep and his trying to get a sneak peak of what jolly ol' St. Nicholas has left for him under the tree. But if that is what Aidan most looks forward to on December 25th, then I will have failed as a father.

And as far as action figures go, Aidan and I are playing with them just about every day, and will continue doing so for about the next two weeks. The ones we play with are hand-painted in Italy. They consist of four sheep, two cows, a donkey, a shepherd, two little children, three angels, three kings, a loving father, a beautiful mother, and a glorious little baby in, as Aidan and I call it, His bed. When we start playing, that baby gets a smile from Aidan that is reserved just for Him. When we're done playing, Aidan kisses that baby and puts Him to bed.

Sharing Christmas with our children requires that we teach them what is most important. It provides us the opportunity to look deep into our own minds and souls and question why we do what we do, and say what we say, and believe what we believe. On a daily basis I am dumbfounded by how difficult it is to try and be a good parent, and I am incredibly hard on myself when I feel I am failing in any of my parental responsibilities. I know there will be days when, for whatever reason, I am not getting the job done as I know it needs to get done.

But in my heart, I know I need to make sure this doesn't ever happen at Christmas. Perhaps that is when Aidan most needs me to be most on top of my game. I owe it to him. I owe it to Tressy. I owe it to his grandparents and the souls of his great-grandparents. And most of all, I owe it to that little baby in the bed.

2003

34 years old

Out of My Hands

I am usually a very sound sleeper. Even after Aidan was born, when I really wanted to be a good father and wake up to do my share when he cried in the middle of the night, it was difficult to wake me out of my deep slumber. But around 3am on July 22nd, Tressy's right elbow crashing down about my chest did the trick.

"Michael!"

My head flew up off the pillow and I sat up at attention with my eyes wide open to the darkness, wondering if a nuclear bomb had landed nearby. And in the next nanosecond, a flood of remembrances rushed across my still-stunned brain… Tressy was at the end of a difficult pregnancy, the baby was breach, and if he or she didn't (against all odds) flip back head down overnight or in the early morning, we were to go to the hospital today and Dr. Armity was going to have to do a C-section.

"The baby!" Tressy screamed. As I turned my head to the left at the speed of light towards the direction of the scream, I saw her face and realized it wasn't a scream of panic or fear. Her hands were gently caressing her belly, and she wore a beautiful animated smile that lit up the darkened room.

"The baby just flipped! I felt it! It woke me up! The baby just flipped!"

"Are you sure? I asked. "How did that happen? Why would that happen?"

"Michael," she said with a calm and confidence that is so wonderfully my wife, "I'm sure."

Yesterday had been a pretty solemn day. When I learned that Tressy was almost certainly going to have to go through major surgery, I was really worried. She had already been through so much adversity during this pregnancy, and after being confined to bed rest for the final few weeks, she was now going to have to go through this as well. I had prayed before going to sleep, asking God to keep Tressy safe and allow our baby to arrive healthy. I was worried that asking for the baby to spin around was asking for too much. So I left it at that. It was out of my hands, and into much more capable ones.

Of course, as she almost always is, Tressy was right. After we arrived at the hospital, her doctor confirmed what she had already known, and we made our way into a labor and delivery room.

Early that evening, we met our daughter and welcomed her into the world.

So here I sit, three weeks before Christmas, Tressy and Aidan out having some holiday fun, and Aria alone with me on the couch. She's on my lap, looking up at me with those huge brown eyes looking like an infant-version of a Japanese anime superhero. She and I are just beginning our relationship, and as she's only 5 months old we're still a ways away from deep and meaningful conversation.

But in our short time together, Aria has already communicated a great deal to me about who she is and who she is going to become. It started with that last minute in utero summersault that saved her mother quite a bit of trauma, and it continues each day with her physicality, her sharp vocalizations, and her boundless energy. This girl may be tiny, but she's powerful. It all has me very excited for her future, but to be honest, it also has me a little bit scared.

Aria was born with a birthmark on her forehead; the kind that normally go away after a few years. Commonly referred to as a stork bite, it is barely noticeable most of the time. But when she's upset, when something in her world is not as she wants it to be, it turns bright red. I consider it my alarm, and when it goes off, I know I have a battle on my hands. And if 5 months is any indicator, I am going to lose a high percentage of those battles.

After much thought and rationalization, I have come to the conclusion that this is yet another example of God giving me what I really need, rather than what would be easy for me. I see lots of fathers who cherish their "daddy's little girl," and often those roles continue into adulthood. I never knew whether I would be blessed with a daughter, but if I was, I knew I never wanted her to be daddy's little girl. Now that I have a daughter, I want her to be her own girl, and to own and be fully responsible for her own identity. And as she grows and develops into a woman, I want her to know that in no way, shape, or form does she remain mine in any significant way. I am struck when men ask their girlfriend's father for his permission to marry his daughter. I will never give such permission, for she is not mine to give.

As I continue to stare into her eyes, and as she looks up into mine with her laser focus, I think about the battles she will fight in the future. Perhaps she will fight for gender equality in the corporate world. Maybe she will go into politics and protect the rights of those who are most vulnerable in our society. Or hopefully be that one friend that so many people turn to when they can't find the strength to defeat a demon and just need someone to have their back, to help carry some of the weight on strong shoulders, and to show them the power of love and faith.

That stork bite will eventually fade away, so her opponents are not going to have any warning that Aria's emotions have been moved to the point of action. I'm not sure they'll ever know what hit them. But I know I will be in her corner, making sure she knows how much I love her, and I will offer her any guidance and wisdom that she asks for and that I can provide.

But I'm not sure how much of my help this little force of nature is going to need. As I eagerly await her first Christmas, and celebrate all the beauty and grace that He brought into our world under that glowing star, I can't help but wonder what profound gifts He has given to Aria that will be revealed in the years to come.

I can sense them. I can feel them. But I don't own them. They are all hers.

And they are out of my hands...

and into much more capable ones.

2004

35 years old

Occhi Santi

Revelation is found in a day's first moment of consciousness. Lying in bed, floating between the dream world and reality, the first image or sound or touch that awakens us often defines the substance and quality of the day that is to follow. This morning, ten days before Christmas, I awoke face-to-face, nose-to-nose, eye-to-eye with the rambunctious four-year-old who, sometime around 3 a.m. most mornings, sneaks into our room and climbs into bed with us. As I blinked repeatedly, and attempted to find my focus through my squinting, I suddenly locked onto those big brown eyes, twinkling like much needed starlight in a dark and empty sky. Moments passed, and he didn't say a word. He just stared, and stared, and stared. And finally, three words, spoken with boundless hope and anticipation: "Is it Christmastime?"

The answer was right there in front of me, shining in his eyes. "Yes, Aidan. It is most definitely Christmastime."

I always dreamed of what it would be like to become a father. As the youngest of five, and with four years between my next-oldest brother, all of my older siblings had children before I was even married. I very much embraced being an uncle to my nieces and nephews, but as much as I loved each of them, I always wondered what it would be like to finally have children of my own. I always imagined looking deep into my son's eyes (for whatever reason, the image was always of a son) and seeing a piece of myself. That dream of seeing myself in my child's eyes stayed with me for years, and I looked forward to fulfilling that dream with great anticipation. But then I had a son. And then I had a daughter. And when that dream became reality, I realized that there was most certainly someone to be found in their eyes. But that someone was not me.

In these troubled times, it can be difficult to focus on the goodness in the world. Casual glances reveal great pain and sorrow, restlessness and division, polarization and fear. In the current social and political climate, we tend to trust "us" and loathe "them," and within this framework there is little impetus for finding common ground; for finding the good that exists in each of us. We now live in a society where there is distance between us, and our interactions with one another most often take place through cell phones, e-mails, and instant messaging. We still talk to one another, but we rarely converse with each other person-to-person, face-to-face, eye-to-eye. Perhaps we find it difficult to find the good in others because we are just too far away to see it.

Tonight, I held Aidan and Aria in my arms, brought them close to my face, and looked deep into their eyes. And I found what I knew I would see. I did not see the conscience of a thirty-five year old man trying his best to face the myriad challenges of life. I saw God.

In their eyes I saw that wondrous twinkle...

the same twinkle that shined down from the heavens above Bethlehem...

the same twinkle that looked at her precious babe lying in the manger...

the same twinkle that gazed up at the star, and at Mary, and that continues to shine brightly in our world...

the same twinkle that you have in your eyes...

now as you read this... and on Christmas morning... and always.

May you and yours have a blessed and joyous Christmas...

and may you see God in the eyes of others...

and may they see God in yours.

2005

36 years old

A Moment In (and Out of) Time

I was eight years old, but I remember the moment like it was yesterday. On November 30, 1977, my maternal grandfather had been rushed to the hospital, and we soon received word that his long struggle with illness was about to end. My brother Joe and I shared a bedroom in those days, and we went to bed that night knowing that our Grandpop was about to die. Sometime in the middle of the night, I laid in bed wide awake. The house was silent, but for a very faint voice somewhere off in the distance. I couldn't identify the voice, or make out what the voice was saying, but I knew that the voice belonged to someone I loved deeply. Despite the fact that nothing remarkable was happening in my dark, quiet bedroom, I knew that something important was happening somewhere else in the world, and I knew that I was very much a part of what was happening, very much a part of something bigger than anything even my childhood imagination could create. I stared up at the ceiling with a consciousness so full it seemed empty, with a mind so full it seemed thoughtless. The seconds, minutes, and hours seemingly rushed past without effect or consequence as the timelessness of the moment enveloped me. It was a moment no words could describe and no time could quantify. And then the moment passed, and I fell asleep.

Again my eyes were open, and again the house was silent. But the sun was now up, and the voice I heard was neither faint nor unrecognizable. It was the voice of my oldest brother, Dominic, whose bedroom was right behind the wall upon which my headboard rested. He was crying, for moments earlier he had been told by my mother that her father had died at 3am. "Are you awake?" Joe asked from his bed across the room. "Yeah," I said. "I think Grandpop died," he said. I said nothing, for there was nothing to say. I had felt it all many hours earlier.

My childhood was punctuated by this moment and a series of others like it...moments when time seemed to stop and I became a part of something much greater than just me. It would be many years before I would be able to articulate the source and significance of those moments, and to acknowledge that they played a prima-ry role in my formation as a man, a Catholic, a husband, and a father. They gave structure and substance to my relationship with the world around me, and connected me to a world within me. In my own mind, they came to define me.

The Ancient Greeks had two different words for time. Chronos is the seconds, minutes, and hours of our days, and is the predecessor of our contemporary western concept of time. It is within Chronos that we wait in line at the post office, creep through traffic to get to work, push our way through layers of pre-recorded phone prompts trying to reach a human voice, etc. Chronos is what it is, and as such, is guided by the unflappable and unchanging laws of physics. It is ordinary time.

But then there are moments that exist outside of ordinary time, moments when the clock seems to stand still and we connect with a power beyond ourselves. These moments are pregnant with opportunity and potential, and serve as poignant reminders of our responsibility to make our world, or at least our little corner of the world, a better place. They inspire even as they comfort, and remind us that even at our loneliest moments we are never alone. These are the moments we live for, and long for, and love for, and eventually die for. This is Kairos. This is sacred time. This is God's time.

As a father of two, I am keenly aware of my countless parental responsibilities. But to me, none are greater than the calling to support Aidan and Aria as they recognize the Sacred and connect with it, and long for it, and be forever moved by it. I am overwhelmed and inspired by how easily they find goodness in the world...how naturally and purely they connect with the Sacred... how willingly they step out of ordinary time.

The Sacred is all around us...in the eyes of our family, in beautiful art that touches our spirit, in the integrity and loyalty of friendship, in the selflessness of sacrifice, in the commitment to serve those in need, in the goodness of a gift given with love. The Sacred is here... waiting for us to find the time, to seize the moment, to step out of time.

For at a moment in time, and at a moment outside of time, a star shined, and a child was born, and heaven came to earth.

At Christmas and always, may we feel that moment in our hearts and souls, and may we long for that feeling each and every day or our lives.

2006

37 years old

AND A LITTLE (ANIMATED) CHILD SHALL LEAD US

The human experience revolves around our search for meaning. This search motivates our most idyllic ambitions and is deeply embedded within our most tragic disappointments.

Perhaps what most excites me about being a parent is the responsibility I now have to introduce the concept of this lifelong search to Aidan and Aria, to develop within them the skills, talents, and virtues to make their quests rich and profound ones, and to share their journeys with them as they grow and experience the ebbs and flows of enlightenment. In my quietest moments, I pray, not only that they will constantly strive to deepen their understanding of our beautifully complex lives, but additionally that they will have the strength to express themselves to the people who make up their little corner of the world, that they will share their faith and hard-earned wisdom with a society so direly in need of both.

This search for meaning that dominates a contemplative life is never more complex than at Christmastime, when we are bombarded daily with temptations to adopt the superficial (and easy) rather than embrace the poignant (and difficult). With so many misguided messages floating around us during our daily interactions, it is a daunting task to surround our children with examples and exemplars of the true spirit of Christmas. In order to help enrich my children's future, I often reach back to my own past to introduce Aidan and Aria to the characters who helped me on my journey when I was a child. These characters may live within the world of literature and the arts, but to me they have always been very real, and their impact on my understanding has been profound. How joyful that, as a father, I now have the opportunity to connect Aidan and Aria with these enlightened souls.

And so I turn to my favorite of all contemporary Christmas tutors, who appears in the most unexpected of places. Linus Van Pelt first appeared in Charles Schulz's comic strip "Peanuts" in 1952. Though he receives far less attention than his best friend, Charlie Brown, his torturous older sister, Lucy, and everyone's favorite beagle, Snoopy, it is Linus whom Schulz most often utilized to convey his own spirituality and faith. Linus is himself a paradox. Though younger than Charlie Brown, he is far past the age when most children stop sucking their thumbs and carrying around their security blankets. But within that seemingly underdeveloped boy lives a very old soul, whose keen intellect is paired with a deep, passionate faith and a quiet courage.

Everyone remembers "A Charlie Brown Christmas" for Charlie's choice of a seemingly pathetic little tree. But it deserves to be remembered for so much more. Charlie Brown has just presented his tree to the cast of the Christmas play. He has been lamenting the commercialization of Christmas and in this humble tree is seeking a far deeper meaning. His hope is soon crushed as the other children harshly ridicule him and his sparse tree. Charlie is distraught, embarrassed, and disappointed by his failed attempt to find a deeper meaning among his peers who clearly see none. Resigned and dejected, he turns to his friend.

"I guess you were right, Linus. I shouldn't have picked this little tree. Everything I do turns into a disaster. I guess I really don't know what Christmas is all about. Isn't there anyone who knows what Christmas is all about?"

And there to fill the silence and answer Charlie's desperate call is Linus. "Sure, Charlie Brown," Linus proclaims with a calm confidence. "I can tell you what Christmas is all about." Linus proceeds to the center of the Christmas play stage, and as the lights dim and the crowd awaits with unparalleled anticipation, he lovingly shares his wisdom. "And there were in the same country shepherds, abiding in the field, keeping watch over their flock by night. And lo, the angel of the Lord came upon them, and the glory of the Lord shone round about them, and they were so afraid. And the angel said unto them 'Fear not for behold I bring you tidings of great joy which shall be to all people. For unto you is born this day in the city of David a Savior, which is Christ the Lord. And this shall be a sign unto you. You shall find the babe wrapped in swaddling clothes lying in a manger.' And suddenly there was with the angel a multitude of the heavenly host praising God and saying, 'Glory to God in the highest, and on earth peace, good will toward men.'"

After a moment's pause, and having delivered the good news, Linus picks up his blanket (which he had surrendered while reciting from Luke's Gospel as the words and images offered safety and security far beyond the abilities of a wool blanket) and turns to his friend. "That's what Christmas is all about, Charlie Brown."

How wonderful it would be if we all had a Linus in our lives to remind us when we most need reminding, to lift our hearts as he lifted Charlie Brown's. Even more, how wonderful it would be if we ourselves could emulate Linus, and we were the ones to fill the silence and to answer the call when our loved ones need us most. That's what Christmas is all about.

Last night, Tressy, Aidan, Aria, and I watched "A Charlie Brown Christmas" for the first time this Christmas season. Aria, with her thumb firmly planted in her mouth and her treasured blanket within her grasp, leapt off of the couch with great excitement when she first saw Linus, with his thumb firmly planted in his mouth and his treasured blanket within his grasp. "Daddy," she proudly proclaimed, "I'm just like him."

With a joy springing from hopes and aspirations Aria is just beginning to understand, I smiled. "Yes you sure are, sweetheart. You're just like him. And that's a wonderful thing to be."

May we all cherish the true meaning of Christmas, and may we possess the courage and faith to proclaim it to our little corners of the world.

2007

38 years old

How Sweet the Sound

In the autumn of 1900 in a small town in northeastern Pennsylvania, Philip Van Doren Stern was born into a family of humble means. When Philip was about my age he had a dream about a man who questioned his own relevance, contemplated suicide after doubting that his existence had positively impacted the world in any way, and was then saved by the grace of God. Philip began recording his dream and over the next few years developed it into a 4,000-word short story, "The Greatest Gift." In December 1943, after failing to get his story published, Philip printed 200 copies, tucked them away inside of his Christmas cards, and sent them to his family and friends.

One of his friends was greatly inspired by Philip's story and shared it with a friend in the movie business. It made its way into the hands of David Hempsted, a producer for RKO Pictures. The movie house purchased Philip's story for $10,000, hoping to make it into a movie. But its screenwriters thrice stumbled in their efforts to adapt it, and the project was scrapped. When RKO received word that a new start-up production company Liberty Films was interested in the story, it cut its losses and sold it for that same $10,000.

Finally, on December 20, 1946, Philip's story, embraced by its new steward Frank Capra, was introduced to the world as a work now recognized as a holiday classic, a genuine slice of early 20th century Americana, and quite simply one of the greatest films of all time: "It's A Wonderful Life."

Most of us have seen this film countless times, and for many its viewing remains a vital Christmas tradition. So much more than just a feel-good holiday movie, the film touches us so deeply because in it we recognize our own search for truth, our own fragility when our search goes awry, and our own humility when we are allowed a glimpse of the Almighty's plan for us.

In our eternal search for meaning, in our perpetual quest to identify the value of our own existence within the great expanse of the cosmos, we celebrate George Bailey's realization that his own life matters greatly, and that without him the world would be much different, and much worse. I have always found it difficult to relate to George Bailey's epiphany, not because of its occurrence, but because of its form. I have no doubt that throughout history God has often worked so directly in people's lives. But I am equally sure that His approach with me has always been more subtle.

I have not yet been visited by a guardian angel who boldly introduces himself as such, and therefore have not been offered the rare sight of what this world might look like if I had never existed. But each day I am visited by the overwhelming and intoxicating beauty of God's grace, and thus I am constantly offered insight into what my world would look like without those who have profoundly impacted my life.

Without my father, I would not know the meaning of hard work. Without my mother, I would not know the meaning of unconditional love. Without Greg Higgins, my high school theology teacher, I would never have discovered the University of Notre Dame, and therefore would never have met Tressy, my partner for all eternity and the woman who gave me Aidan and Aria. Without Aidan and Aria, my window to God's grace would never have opened so wide.

And without the man (whose name I do not know) who sold my paternal grandfather a chestnut farm in Italy in 1946, my grandfather would have had to purchase a farm from someone else. That other farm would not have contained chestnuts infected with a one-in-one-hundred-year plague, my grandfather's entire first crop would not have spoiled before ever making it to market, my grandfather would not have lost his entire investment and been forced to return to America (bringing my father and his siblings with him), my father would never have met my mother, and I would have never been born.

So whether we arrive directly or indirectly, with the intercession of a guardian angel or with the contemplation of an ever-curious mind, George Bailey and I each come to Christmas humbled by the enormity of our blessings, awe struck by the generosity of our loved ones, and overwhelmed by the presence of the One who gives meaning to us all.

May your Christmas be filled with perspective, with thanksgiving, and with God's grace that rains down upon us each day and promises eternity on the most silent of nights.

2008

39 years old

MES DAMES

In any other year, the morning of December 10th would likely be a pretty happy time. Tressy and I would wake up around 5 am, turn on the lights of our Christmas tree, and enjoy the soft glowing illumination of our Christmas decorations. While enjoying a hot cup of Christmas tea and a bowl of Honey Bunches of Oats, I'd eventually hear the pitter-patter of two sets of feet and shortly thereafter see Aidan's and Aria's little faces appear from behind the stairwell. Thanks to the internet and my uber-organized wife, most of our Christmas shopping would be completed. We would have finalized babysitting arrangements for Christmas parties, and finalized the menu for a holiday breakfast for friends and neighbors. All organized. All according to plan.

But this year December 10th was a bit different. At 5

am I was sitting alone in the tiny chapel of Jersey Shore University Medical Center. In my left hand was a prayer card for Santa Margherita I had purchased for my mother a few years back, and which had been tucked safely underneath the visor of her car until the night before. In my right hand was a beautiful new rosary I had recently received from a dear friend, and which had been blessed the day before by my parents' pastor. Four floors above me, my mother was being prepped for open heart surgery. I was sitting alone. But I was not alone. My ladies were with me.

As I prayed the rosary, my mind kept flashing before me countless memories with my mom, a lifetime of individual moments of love, of care, and of protection.

Like that humid, summer day in 1988 when my mom and I stood at the main entrance of the University of Notre Dame, shielding our eyes from the brilliantly blinding sight before us. I was trying to decide where to go to college, and we decided to make a special trip to Notre Dame to understand what it was all about. As we gazed up at the statue of the Blessed Virgin Mary, gleaming atop her Golden Dome and keeping watch over her university, we both knew we had found what I, and we, were looking for.

A few months later, with freshman orientation completed and my parents' departure just moments away, I hugged and kissed my mother goodbye, and with tears in my eyes, turned to walk away. As I turned my eyes skyward, again there was Mary on the Dome, looking down upon me. I knew that in a few moments my mother would be gone, soon far away, but I also knew that I would not be without a mother's love, without a mother's care, without a mother's protection. My ladies were with me then too.

Like that gray winter day in 1994 when, instead of preparing for my law school exams, I was across the river in a different hospital, having a quiet conversation with my mom while my dad underwent his own open heart surgery. I remember how calm she appeared to be, and how I knew I had no reason to doubt her when she assured me that everything was going to be alright. His surgery was on December 8th, the feast day of the Immaculate Conception of Mary. My ladies were with me then too.

So I guess I shouldn't have been surprised when three weeks ago, as a catheterization revealed two heart valves in need of repair and a blocked major artery in need of a bypass, my mom's team of doctors initially scheduled her surgery for that very same feast day. And I guess I shouldn't have been surprised when I learned that the surgeon who was going to be performing this highly complex series of procedures was a fellow alumnus of Notre Dame, of Our Lady's university. I'm sure many will point to all of these things as a series of coincidences, as rationalizations of my own mind as I attempted to deal with this tremendously stressful situation.

But I know the truth. I know that two thousand years ago, a faithful young girl was engaged to a humble carpenter when an archangel appeared and delivered the shocking and world-altering news that God was with her. She was to give birth to a son, a son who would be the world's salvation. I know that girl was doubted by her community, outcast by her friends, and ridiculed as deceitful and impure. And I know the unparalleled strength she demonstrated in carrying that unbearable weight, on delivering on the most sacred of promises. I know she understood how much her son would mean to the world. And as I clutched that rosary tighter and tighter, I knew she understood what my mother means to me, and what I mean to her.

Five hours later, as her surgeon relayed to us that the surgery had gone exceptionally well and that we could see her in a few minutes, I closed my eyes and could hear my mother's voice in my head and heart, again telling me that everything would be alright. With my rosary still in my hands, I knew my ladies were with me. I knew that Christmas was coming.

May your Christmas be touched by the ladies in your life, by the love offered only by their hearts, and with the strength found only in their spirit.

2009

40 years old

(Un)Blinded by the Light

I'm sitting at my desk staring out the window, eyes transfixed on the last remnants of the Arizona winter sun as it blazes a trail of reds and oranges across the ever-blackening sky. Minute by minute, second by second, the intensity of the colors fade away into an increasingly expansive blanket of darkness. In a few minutes all of the color will sink away behind the mountains, beyond the curvature of the earth, and I will be left with the blackness of the evening sky. It will come, and sadly, it will feel all too familiar.

These are dark times, for our world and its economies, for our country and its spirit, for our friends and family and our daily struggles. The news is a constant stream of war, foreclosures, infidelity, corporate greed, violence, sadness, unemployment, and disease, and there isn't a single one of us who hasn't been touched, directly or indirectly, by the depth and breadth of the darkness.

But it is at this particular time in our shared history when we must remember that a light shines brightest during the darkest of nights. So it was two millennia ago. So it is now.

I imagine it was on a night like tonight that it first appeared. In a blackened sky that absorbed all of the world's trouble and sorrow, it emerged in the sky. At first it was a curiosity, a light outshining all other lights in the sky. Pragmatic explanations were given for its sudden arrival, while sensible expectations were created to defend its expected equally-sudden departure. But those explanations rang hollow, and the sudden departure never came. The light was calling. Its allure became irresistible, for what it offered was needed so very badly. It offered hope where there had been no hope… the potential for love… the promise of life. And so they left behind all that they were to search for all that they could become. Kings and shepherds, those who were willing to risk it all and those who had nothing to risk… they allowed themselves to be guided by the light. They traveled to the ends of the earth and beyond, with faith that the light would guide them to answers… to something greater than what they had known.

And so during these dark days we search, each of us, for the light that will guide us to love… that will guide us to life. That light is the source of our daily motivation. It's why we wake up in the morning; it's our doorway to the world's grace; its our raison d'etre; it's our reason for even wanting to be. And chances are it is right in front of us. If we allow it to guide us, it will lead us to where we long to be.

For the past twenty years, I have had the blessing and honor of having that light shine on me each and every day, not from across the universe, but from much closer range. We all have a physical embodiment of that light that shows us the way when the way is so hard to find. For some it is a father, a mother, a sibling, a son, a daughter, a friend. For me, it is my wife. I have met thousands of people in my lifetime, but somewhere deep down in Tressy's core is an energy and goodness that outshines all else I have seen in my forty years. Because of her I strive to be a better man, a better father, a better son, a better friend. In her eyes is a reflection of who I want to be, who I know I can someday become. In her tenderness is the perfect example of what Aidan and Aria need most from me, which isn't always what is easiest for me to give. In her wisdom is the reminder that my side of the story is never the whole side of the story. In her love is the acceptance of my shortcomings, and an offer of hope and redemption that tomorrow will be better than today. She is my guide to a better me... to a better us... to a better life.

Like the star that led countless sojourners so many years ago, she leads me to all that is oh so very right in the world. Like that star, she leads me to God.

May you embrace the light that guides you through your darkest of nights, and may it lead you to the joy and love and promise of Christmas.

2010

41 years old

A World Transformed

This summer I was helping a friend and colleague redesign her office space. I was in the process of conceptualizing some bold signage for behind her reception area, and as her focus is on international law, I excitedly suggested that we could superimpose a world map on top of a brushed stainless steel representation of her university's logo. She loved the idea. So I asked a cutting-edge graphics company to produce a rendering for me, and then emailed the rendering to my friend. "I like it," she said, "but have you ever heard of Peters Projection Map?"

I asked her to explain. She sent me links to a few websites, a handful of articles, and a YouTube link to an episode of The West Wing that touched upon this topic. In it, representatives from the Organization of Cartographers for Social Equality come to the White House to make a presentation urging the President to require that all American public schools replace the Mercator Projection Map with the Peters Projection Map.

The cartographer Gerardus Mercator created his map in 1569 with the intention of helping explorers navigate the seas. And indeed, its straight lines of latitude and longitude greatly assisted seafarers in getting from point A to point B. The imagery presented on this map is what most of us westerners know as "the world," and as such, the map still hangs in many classrooms, fills pages in many textbooks, and is the default image of the planet earth for many entities worldwide. The problem is… well, it's just wrong. It's woefully inaccurate. It greatly inflates the areas closest to the poles and horribly distorts the size and location of landmasses.

Created as a response to this inaccuracy, Peters Projection Map, first unveiled in 1974 by Arno Peters, much more accurately depicts the size and location of the earth's lands. This map has fidelity of axis and position and portrays the world much differently than we are used to, but much closer to how it really is. In reality, Greenland is fourteen times smaller than it appears on Mercator's map. South America is twice as big. Africa, in reality, is large… very, very, very large. And northern Europe, not coincidentally Mercator's homeland, is not really in the center of the world as he portrays it, but is actually a small area tucked away near the top of the northern hemisphere.

In altering our sense of reality, Peters Projection Map teaches us an important lesson about our planet. If we refocus our eyes and open our minds, we learn that nothing is the size and shape we think it is. And nothing is where we think it is. And perhaps, nothing is what we think it is.

And so we arrive at a series of questions: what if humanity has already been given a Peters Projection Map, not for the planet, but for our lives? What if the elemental people, concepts, and standards within our lives suddenly shifted meaning… suddenly were something other than what we always thought they were? What if we learned that the little moments in life that constantly and consistently drift by us unnoticed actually have meaning beyond comprehension? What if we discovered, in a moment, that life isn't what we thought it was? And in that very same moment, what if we discovered that life is something infinitely greater… infinitely richer... infinitely more meaningful?

Christmas offers us that moment, not just once, but over and over again for all eternity. In the twinkle of a wondrous baby's eye, we are given a map of perfect clarity and precision, a vision of our greatest version of ourselves and the love and joy we deserve to experience each day. In the boundless love of a miraculous young mother, we are challenged to find the patience and grace that can utterly transform our daily lives if we learn to let them. In the humility of the three who were wise among wise, we are motivated to ignore all the reasons we invent to put ourselves first and instead bow down and recognize the dignity and beauty in those whom society deems last. And in a shining star, we are blessed with a perpetual beacon to guide us through the darkness that exists in some corner of all our hearts, leading us to a world of infinite beauty... infinite passion... infinite love... and infinite life.

Our Peters Projection Map is Christmas. Christmas is our gift. Our gift is Him.

This Christmas, may you see your life as it really is, and may you use this insight to spend each day seeking beauty, giving love, and celebrating all that you are and hope to be.

2011

42 years old

A (NOTRE DAME) MAN AMONG (NOTRE DAME) MEN

Every fall, as the weather begins to cool and the sun begins to sink below the horizon ever earlier, Aidan and I take a long weekend trip together to Notre Dame. He misses two days of school (something Tressy and I do not take lightly) and I stop answering email and put my work on the back burner (something I take even less lightly). It is a time of incredible connection filled with a series of special moments, and like all things in this world that I truly cherish, considered by us both to be sacred time.

Like most ritualistic behavior, the four-day agenda is strikingly constant. We arrive in Chicago on Thursday afternoon and drive for 90 minutes to South Bend. We make the ceremonial drive up Notre Dame Avenue approaching the Golden Dome, and after spending some

time praying at the Grotto and relishing in our breath-
takingly beautiful campus, we attend a cultural event at
the performing arts center. Friday we meet up with my
best friend, Bob, and his son, Justin, and spend the day
playing football on South Quad, celebrating our friend-
ships. Saturday, of course, is all about the pageantry
and drama of Notre Dame football, and Saturday night
is pizza at Bruno's. Sunday morning delivers the timeless gift of Mass at the Basilica, where Tressy and I took
our vows and the place on this planet where I feel most
connected to God. After the melancholy departing drive
down Notre Dame Avenue, with the Golden Dome now
in the rear view mirror, we return to Chicago to catch our
plane back to Arizona. The trip is sublime and as close to
perfect as anything in my world. But sometime (fearfully
soon) the trip will change, and I am not sure how I will
be able to cope with the new reality.

Among all the other gifts it bestows upon Aidan and
me, our annual pilgrimage to Notre Dame is the one
time each year I have the opportunity to visit Father Al
D'Alonzo. I first met Fr. Al my sophomore year when he
came to live with us in Pangborn Hall as our Assistant
Rector. I was immediately drawn to him. Then in his six-
ties, it took little time to realize he was very intelligent,
very opinionated, very Italian, and very much from the
great state of New Jersey. It was clear we were going to
hit it off quite well.

But what was more difficult to understand is what
I have learned in the 22 years since then. In college, I
spent countless hours in Fr. Al's room, conversing

about all that matters in life from family and friendship to Aquinas and Verdi. We went to Italian restaurants and ate richly-sauced gnocchi and drank lots of Chianti. We walked around campus and commented on the architecture of the buildings and of the trees. We studied the Bible together. We prayed together. We cursed about the shortcomings of Notre Dame football together. While in law school in New York City, we spoke by phone every few weeks, and my visits with him quickly became the highlight of my football weekend returns to campus. Upon my law school graduation, we flew to Italy together and for 3 weeks he graciously introduced me to the land and culture of my ancestors. He was there for me to celebrate our wedding Mass and to baptize Aidan and Aria into the Faith. I was there for him to celebrate his 50th anniversary of his priesthood within the order of the Holy Cross. My family became his family. His family became mine.

He is a man unlike any other I have met, a man who is needed now more than ever in a world desperately searching for role models and heroes. He is not a moral compass; he is the moral compass. He is my daily reminder and the universe's most ferocious advocate that there is moral objectivity in the world, and that certain ideas and principles are inherently good and not just matters of opinion. He is unwavering in his faith. He is unflappable in his commitment to serve others. He is all that a priest should be. He is all that a man should be. But time has done what it always does; it has moved forward. Father Al has grown old, his strength and eyesight have left him, and whenever my cell phone receives a call from area code 574, I am afraid to answer it.

I write these words here with full acknowledgment of the awkwardness of the situation. I will be sending these words to Fr. Al in his Christmas card, and I expect his family will read them to him. I understand that such words are usually reserved for after someone has moved on and has been reunited with the Almighty. But these words cannot wait. These words need to be expressed now, and expressed publicly.

Two months ago, on the Sunday of our annual Notre Dame trip, Aidan and I went to visit Fr. Al in the nursing home that houses those Holy Cross priests and religious who are in the twilight of their years. Before we went, I had a very honest conversation with Aidan and warned him that Fr. Al wasn't going to be like Aidan remembered him, and gave him the option of staying in the lobby if he thought it would be too difficult. As I knew he would, Aidan insisted on being by my side.

We walked into the room and Fr. Al was lying in bed with his eyes closed. He had changed so much since I had seen him last. I put down the cannoli we had brought him, kneeled by his bedside, and grabbed his hands with both of mine. "Fr. Al, it's Michael." His eyes remained shut, but I knew he instantly recognized my voice. Over the next 10 minutes his eyes stayed closed, but he smiled and commented warmly as I recalled for him so many of our adventures. I was walking him through the many years of our friendship, and it became painfully clear that this would likely be the last time I would see him on this earth.

"Someone's here with me. Aidan's here too." I pulled Aidan close to me, my eyes now so filled with tears that I could barely recognize my own son. But I could clearly see that Fr. Al's eyes then opened, and he reached out his hand for Aidan's, and over the next five minutes the Spirit moved within him and his face lit up with light and energy. I shared with him how much he meant to me and how he forever changed the way I would live my life. I told him he was my life teacher, and that he was now teaching Aidan about life and death and how to move through moments of transformation with grace and dignity. Both squeezed my hands tightly, and a tear rolled down Father Al's cheek. It was the first time I had ever seen him cry.

We fully understood what was happening. We were not just saying goodbye, we were saying thank you for all the joy we had shared, thank you for all the blessings and time we had been given, thank you for the gift of having such a remarkable person grace our life's journey. Fr. Al offered Aidan a blessing in perfect Latin, smiled, touched Aidan's cheek, and then touched mine. He gazed up into my eyes, and I gazed into his. "I love you, Fr. Al. Get some rest." The feeling in that room was proof enough of God's existence. I will never forget it.

Time moves so quickly, and we never know what is going to happen in the next moment. I still have so much to learn, about life, about love, and about how to live each moment giving those around me the respect and affection they deserve. I needed to tell Fr. Al what he is and has been in my life, just like I need to share words of gratitude with all of you.

This Christmas, as I ponder all that was given on that starriest of nights and all that would be sacrificed for us, I will also cherish the impact so many of you have had in my life. Our lives are a beautiful and continual tapestry of moments, and mine is made of the threads and patterns of all of you. It is my sincere wish that you treasure each of these moments, this Christmas and always, and that you recognize the beauty that surrounds us... now and forever.

2012

43 years old

2012

43 years old

And Now I Know Why

Less than seven weeks after Hurricane Sandy ravaged the northeast, a different kind of storm, one of unimaginable horror, has not only devastated a small town in Connecticut, but threatens to tear apart the heart and soul of a nation. As these negative events tempt our anger and frustration, we must not allow the tempest to bring out the very worst in us. Instead, as we pray for the families of those whose children and loved ones will not be with them this Christmas, our genuine outpouring of love and support for those in pain reveals the very best in us.

As Aidan's and Aria's father, I feel a strong responsibility to help them develop the navigational tools to guide them successfully above and around the walls of negativity our nature all too often constructs. I pray that they choose to swim against the tide, and that they reverse the polarity of our emotional and psychological magnet. I want them to be drawn to the positive. I want to teach them to believe that we are more than just our neurological wiring. I want to guide them and travel alongside them on a journey beyond what we have been to what we are capable of being. And I want to motivate them to seek out those in the world who are on this same courageous journey, and when they find them, to embrace them, to celebrate them, to cherish them.

Manti Te'o's journey took an unexpected turn four years ago. As one of the best high school football players in America and arguably the best to ever come from Hawaii, he received scholarship offers from top universities across the country. He could have chosen the University of Hawaii and remained in his island paradise and close to his parents and family. He could have chosen Brigham Young University where 98% of his fellow students would have shared the LDS faith that sustains him. He could have chosen his childhood favorite University of Southern California, which had won 46 of 52 games over the past four seasons. But Manti made a different choice.

On 22 November 2008, he boarded a plane to travel east of California for the first time. He landed in South Bend, Indiana wearing shorts and flip-flops, unprepared for the 18-degree temperatures and blanketing snow. He was even less prepared when he witnessed the Irish lose at home to a lowly 2-9 Syracuse team that had just fired its head coach a week prior. The weather was so bad that he watched most of the second half on television in the locker room, witnessing a disgusted and forlorn student body tossing snowballs onto the field after the embarrassing loss.

Manti's official recruiting visit could not have been more negative. So when Manti chose to attend the University of Notre Dame, everyone, including his parents and family, was surprised. As a young man of deep faith, Manti had prayed for guidance in making what he knew would be a lifelong decision. "My dad always told me, the hardest thing when asking the Lord for advice is not necessarily getting on your knees and praying, but having the courage to follow through with the answer that you receive. At that time, I was a USC fan; I wanted to go to USC. The answer I felt to come here to Notre Dame wasn't the answer I anticipated, and wasn't the one I wanted."

When Manti arrived on campus, five thousand miles from home, he was incredibly homesick and believed that time would tell whether he had made the right decision. After three very strong but not exceptional seasons, when he turned down big money from the NFL to return to Notre Dame for his senior year, he explained that he measured himself by the impact he had on other people, that he had been called to Notre Dame to make a difference in people's lives, and that he still had work to do at Notre Dame.

This year, in leading Notre Dame to a perfect 12-0 season, Manti has become in many people's view the best player in college football. But his story transcended sport when on that September day he learned his beloved grandmother had died, and then, just hours later, he lost his girlfriend to leukemia. In the days, weeks, and months that followed, Manti displayed, both privately and publicly, the strength of character and spirit of humility that we all wish we could exhibit when our harshest of storms bear down upon us. In the face of the unthinkable, this remarkable man became an even better leader, an even more loyal friend, an even more loving son, and an even better football player. In the face of the unthinkable, Manti touched a nation, and became a beacon of goodness and humility to millions around the country, including my family. In delivering his best when the storm was the worst, he did what he had come back to do. The day before his girlfriend's funeral, the day before he played the best game of his life as she made him promise he would if something happened to her, in front of a silent mass of thousands of Notre Dame students professing their love and support by wearing Hawaiian leis and holding up his #5 with their fingers, Manti Te'o now understood the answer to his prayers. "Four years ago I made a decision to come here to Notre Dame and I didn't really know why. And now I know why."

We are bombarded each day with news of horrible and disturbing events happening all around us. We are defined by how we handle these moments of adversity, by how we respond when in the midst of our storms.

On the profile page of Manti Te'o's Twitter account, he doesn't present himself as the record-setting, award-winning linebacker that he is. He doesn't allude to the upcoming national championship game, his Sports Illustrated cover, or his almost certain NFL stardom. Instead, Manti chooses to quote Alexandre Dumas: "Life is a storm. You will bask in the sunlight one moment, be shattered on the rocks the next. What makes you a man is what you do when that storm comes."

As I sit in awe of Manti's faith, I consider the faith of another, of the one whose likeness looks over her and our university from atop the Golden Dome. In humbly accepting the mission of bringing God into our human world, Mary felt the life-giving warmth of the sun yet understood that the storm would come far too soon to take that life away. She comprehended the overwhelming suffering her child was destined to endure, and the unthinkable pain she would feel witnessing it all play out before her eyes and upon her heart. But Mary trusted that putting her faith in a power far greater than herself would give her the courage to carry and deliver that wondrous baby, to withstand the most violent of all storms, and to save the world.

This Christmas, I am so thankful that Manti Te'o has provided Aidan and Aria, along with Tressy, me, and millions of others, a beautiful testament to the trusting of faith, the necessity of humility, and the saving power of love.

May we all strive to be our best when our storms are at their worst, and with faith, humility, and love, may we all make a difference in the lives of those around us and thereby save our own little corner of the world.

2013

44 years old

Until Next Year

There are certain feelings not expressed in Hallmark Christmas cards. They are not the focus of Coca-Cola holiday ads. They are not featured live onstage during the Radio City Music Hall Christmas Spectacular. They are not the topics of songs on Mary J. Blige's and Kelly Clarkson's new Christmas albums.

You are likely about to celebrate Christmas with a wonderful meal, surrounded by family and friends, with presents tucked under a beautiful Christmas tree. It should be a very Merry Christmas indeed.

But for many, for far too many that our collective conscience should allow, Christmas will be a radically difference experience. While we ponder whether to have a second helping of chocolate cherry bread pudding, others will be shielding their faces from the wind as they stand in a long line waiting to receive that day's lone meal. While we are giddy with anticipation to tear through the wrapping paper holding that special present from our spouse, others are shrouded in apprehension, praying desperately that today might be an exception and their spouse's anger won't flare up and leave another bruise. While our children are nestled in their warm beds dreaming of Santa's arrival, others will be hoping for a thicker blanket as they try to fall asleep, shivering in the darkness. As we walk into Mass looking dapper and lovely in our cashmere and wool, others spend another day avoiding a mirror that offers a harsh reminder of the damage caused by illness, disease, and misfortune.

Christmas is not always Merry. And though the dichotomy of experience between the fortunate and the less fortunate is disquieting, it is also quite real. This reality becomes our own once we come to understand that the difference between "us" and "them" is a fiction. And one remarkable man is boldly and courageously piercing the veil of that fiction and opening our hearts, minds, eyes, and souls to the real story.

Jorge Mario Bergoglio never aspired to be Pope. But as Pope Francis, he clearly wants us all to become better versions of ourselves. From his choice of name nine months ago to his choice of inviting homeless men to share his birthday with him a few days ago, he is a manifestation of seeing others in ourselves, a model of understanding, selflessness, and humility. He chooses to live in a guest house at the Vatican instead of the papal apartment and drives in a used car instead of the papal Mercedes. He sent Christmas presents to two thousand immigrants at a shelter near the Vatican. During general audiences, he crosses barricades and goes into the crowd to personally connect with children with disabilities. He got on his knees and washed the feet of young female, Muslim prisoners. He hugged and kissed a man so scarred and deformed by a genetic abnormality that he is regularly mocked by strangers. After receiving a letter from a woman who had been raped, he picked up the phone and called her so she would know that she was not alone. He regularly sneaks out of the Vatican at night, wearing the simple black clerics and white collar of a parish priest, to meet and serve the homeless.

And his glorious words (whether they be in official papal documents, mainstream television news interviews, or tweets) make it unmistakably clear that Pope Francis inspires hundreds of millions of people around the world, not to redefine that which defines us, but to intensify our focus on the part of that definition that matters most: the Church must stand as an example of compassion for those in need, of forgiveness for those who have lost their way, and of love for each and every one of us.

Pope Francis embraces change, while still insisting upon truth. These ideals strongly resonate with me. I have always tried to live my life believing that principles matter, knowing that objective truth exists, and that seeking it is a critical component of trying to live a good life. And professionally, I have utilized these ideals to build a reputation as a change agent, a futurist, and an aspirational thinker and doer.

But the last year has been a difficult one for me, for unforeseen circumstances have led me to question a critical part of what defines me. Embracing change while insisting upon truth has alienated me from some of the very people who have given my life shape and structure. It has put into question some of the relationships that have contextualized my journey. It has led to many sleepless nights. It has made it very difficult to finish the words you are reading, and has brought me to the first Christmas of my life that does not feel very Merry.

I needed Pope Francis this year. I need him now. At a time when I am questioning that which I never needed to question, he is revealing answers that will almost certainly change my focus. He is a daily reminder that in my darkest moments, I am still so very fortunate.

And I needed my wife this year. I need her now. Yesterday she knew my spirit needed to be lifted, and knowing Pope Francis has been touching my heart, she shared with me the following words from the Prayer of St. Francis…

"Lord, make me an instrument of your peace. Where there is hatred, let me sow love. Where there is injury, pardon. Where there is doubt, faith. Where there is despair, hope. Where there is darkness, light. Where there is sadness, joy."

And so this year, I will pray for a Christmas… graced with pardon, grounded in faith, inspired by hope, bathed in light, and, as all things should be, full of love.

The joy will have to wait until next year.

2014

45 years old

Our Christmas Present to Lily

I am not a big fan of Christmas presents. This radical claim has been the source of great angst throughout my adult life, and has led to many a disagreement with the ones I most love. It's not that I don't appreciate gift giving. In fact, I believe giving someone a personal and thoughtful gift is a beautiful expression of love. My issue lies with the secularization of a sacred season, and with the ideology that celebrating Christmas should revolve around shiny boxes and big red bows.

And so I am myself surprised to discover that as Christmas approaches this year, I am almost singularly focused on a Christmas present. I barely knew its intended recipient. In fact, we have only been in the same room twice before. But I believe she will embrace this

Christmas present. And one day, when I meet her again, she will share how much this gift means to her.

I first met Lily at my parents' home on Christmas Eve fifteen years ago. My paternal grandfather died three months before I was born, but my father often told me that Domenico would frequently invite new friends to his home to celebrate the Feast of the Seven Fishes on Christmas Eve. My dear friend Jeff had recently fallen in love with Sharena, a beautiful woman from Trinidad who had, just 3 months earlier, brought 8-year-old Lily to the US. So in the spirit of my grandfather, I invited Jeff and his new family to join us at my parents' home, and Jeff graciously accepted.

Only last month did I learn how much that night so many years ago meant to Lily. As is almost always the case in life, things were much more complex than they seemed. I know now that Lily had seen and felt far more and far worse than a young girl should see and feel. Her biological father had habitually abused her mother in front of her eyes, and once his wrath had ceased and he had left the scene, Lily would literally kiss her mother wounds in an effort to console her. Sharena had come to this country as an escape from the violence. She came seeking kindness and compassion and the opportunity to create a new and better life for herself and her children, who she vowed to bring to the US as soon as she was able.

Lily came here as an outsider; her skin darker than those around her, her accent revealing that she was from "somewhere else." I remember her staying so very close to her mother's side that night, but I was clueless how uncertain and frightened she must have been. Everything in this country was new and foreign, and here she was at a stranger's house surrounded by people she didn't know and, justifiably considering her life experience, had no reason to trust.

So when a right jolly old elf with a snow white beard bound through the front door with a giant sack full of presents, the last thing in the world she expected was that there might be something in that bag for her. The world just didn't work that way. And so it took her by surprise, in the most wonderfully healing of ways, when Santa exuberantly called out her name. She found the courage to leave her mother's side and approached the gift giver, who was reaching towards her with a large package wrapped in shiny paper and tied up in a big red bow. She returned to her mother's side and tore open the gift, bewildered by how he could have known about the roller blades she had wished for, and in her size, no less. In a moment, Lily found connection… she found acceptance… she found affirmation… she found hope. And there behind the scene, quietly watching every moment, his eyes full of tears that ran down his face and across his beaming smile, was the source of it all… my friend Jeff.

As she grew into a young woman, Lily moved through the world with an energy and spirit that could brighten any room, lighten any mood, warm the coldest of hearts, and turn any frown upside down. Jeff not only became Lily's father, he became her confidant, her buddy, her jokester, and her trusted friend. Lily became the light of his life.

But life is more complex than it seems. The wounds of our early years may eventually heal, but they leave behind scars that stay with us every day of our lives. Like so many young people who have been exposed to the dirty ways of the world, Lily was unable to find for herself the peace and happiness that she so easily brought to others. Her life's peaks and valleys became more extreme, and the light she shined so brightly onto the world could not protect her from the internal darkness that haunts so many of us.

One month before the end of her freshman year of college, Lily sank into a deep depression. She had just broken up with her boyfriend and nothing seemed to be going well in her life. Jeff and Sharena were there for her, and had been getting her help. Both they and her friends believed Lily was out of harm's way. She promised them she wouldn't do anything drastic.

And so when Lily sent a text to Jeff and posted a message on social media that sounded an alarm, Jeff frantically tried to find her. Their Jersey Shore community had been tragically impacted by a suicide cluster, a continuing and systemic series of teenage suicides, many of which occurred by putting themselves in the way of an oncoming train. Through sobs of fear, Jeff raced in his car from train station to train station, trying to reach her by cell phone, needing to let her know that hope never dies, and that once she got past the pain of these difficult days, the world would reopen to her.

His phone rang. It was Lily's sister. She told Jeff he needed to come home; it was the worst of news. Lily had driven her car onto the railroad tracks. The oncoming train tried to stop in time; it couldn't. The darkness got too dark.

Three and a half years later, Jeff and Sharena are still trying to make sense of it all. The pain will never go away. But despite the immeasurable sadness, Jeff is determined to deliver that message that he never had the chance to communicate to Lily. In her memory, Jeff wants to help save the lives of other young people who are fighting the darkness that Lily bravely fought. He wants to save other parents from suffering through the irreplaceable loss that no parent should experience.

My friend reached out to me, asking if I might think and pray about how we could help those who are struggling. Prayers were answered, and through a remarkable series of events that can only be explained by divine providence, we have recruited a superstar team of talented and compassionate friends and are making Jeff's dream a reality. This mission has become our passion and purpose.

Soon we will be launching, through a nationwide campaign, an innovative smartphone app specifically designed to save lives, relying on psychological best practices and technological prowess. My Help Button will empower young people, at a moment of calm long before dark storm clouds start forming, to create a support team of friends, family, and mentors. Then, if a moment of crisis occurs, one click on their phone will automatically notify their team that immediate help, love, and support are needed. The team will instantaneously receive the location of the person in need, and together strive to help avert a tragedy and save a precious life.

This all-important project is the final piece of our Christmas present to Lily. It is the culmination of a gift that began with a smile from Santa, a calling of her name, a shiny box, and a pair of rollerblades. By channeling her spirit and embracing her soul, together we will help countless numbers of young people... to be there for them at their time of greatest need... and help them find connection... find acceptance... find affirmation... find hope... and reach the next and best chapter of their lives.

The inspiring and brilliant Canadian poet Shane Koyczan recently penned, "If you think for one second no one knows what you've been going through; be accepting of the fact that you are wrong, that the long drawn and heavy breaths of despair have at times been felt by everyone - that pain is part of the human condition, and that alone makes you a legion."

After all, isn't that what Christmas is all about? God humbled himself and became one of us to let us know that we are not alone... to assure us that even in our darkest moments, even when hope seems as distant as the faintest star, we can trust Him and trust each other, knowing that the star of hope will shine brightly once again.

2015

46 years old

Keeping My Promise

Christmas is coming. It is two weeks away. I am standing at the top of the world, on the precipice of the highest watchtower along the Jingshangling stretch of the iconic Great Wall of China. There are no words for such a view. The slightest turn of my head reveals another hundred miles of snow-covered mountains, along with the hidden ghosts of centuries and millennia past. I strain to hear their voices in the near absolute silence. I am alone. It is cold. Christmas is coming. And I am listening for the voice of Aunt Lou.

My Aunt Louise was one of a kind. Though 14 years older than my father, I never associated her with her age, or for that matter, with any age. She was beyond age. She was timeless.

I thought this mostly because Aunt Lou had a passion for life that was always, not only palpable, but also beautifully contagious. You could not be in her presence without her energy wrapping itself around you and pulling you close to her. When any of us in her large extended family (which extended far beyond Bossone blood to the realm of almost anyone she ever met) was lucky enough to be with her, we felt recognized... we felt appreciated... we felt loved.

Her compassion and kindness were limitless. But all that selflessness was wrapped up in a package of spitfire and sass. She knew where she stood in this world and held her ground with principle and determination. She may not have been fearless, but she never let fear keep her from revealing her true and authentic self. If I asked Aunt Lou a question, I always knew I would get an honest answer, even (and more importantly especially) if it wasn't what I wanted to hear, but was what I needed to hear. She could instantly awaken me from a moral or emotional slumber with a verbal slap in the face, and then immediately follow it with a physical kiss on the cheek.

All of these thoughts and hundreds like them were ricocheting across my mind as I boarded a plane with my family this past 27 February for a 3-day cross-country trip. Tressy, Aidan, Aria, and I had recently learned that the cancer had spread to her bones, and that time was catching up with my beloved and timeless Aunt Lou. We were flying to New Jersey to face reality. We were flying to New Jersey to say goodbye.

When we walked into her home, you could feel that time was running out. I could see it in my sister's face as she greeted us warmly at the front door. It became overwhelming when we rounded the corner of the living room and saw Aunt Lou sitting in her chair.

One by one we embraced her ever so tenderly, and after Tressy and the kids each had their priceless moments alone with her, Tressy guided everyone out of the room so that Aunt Lou and I could be alone.

There are so many decisions to make when someone you love is dying. Each and every one of them is difficult, and sadly, many cause years of regret and second-guessing among the surviving. There was great uncertainty as to whether or not Aunt Lou understood that she had only a few days to live, and an uncertainty as to whether anyone should ask her if she knew what was happening. With great respect for the differences of opinion, and for the various opinion holders, I already knew I was going to ask her. I honored her by staying true to the authenticity of our treasured relationship. I would ask her a question, and I knew I would get an honest answer.

I gazed into her eyes. We gently smiled to each other as I caressed her right hand as it rested in both of mine. She was fully there. She was tired. She was in pain. But she was fully there.

My words broke the long and sacred silence. "How bad is it?"

Her reply was immediate, and in the language of her beloved mother, whom I had kneeled before and whose hand I had caressed years earlier in this very same home.

In a purposefully soft voice, without any hint of disappointment, discontent, or fear, she confirmed what I already knew in my heart.

"Finito." Finished. Completed. Done.

We talked then about what a beautiful life she had lived, and about all of the lives she had touched and made better by sharing her love and kindness. I thanked her for the profound impact she had on me, and assured her that I would carry with me each and every day all of the life lessons she taught me. She assured me that she wasn't afraid of death and was ready to be reunited with her family and friends. She knew her mother was ready to welcome her.

There was one last question I needed to ask Aunt Lou before I left. Her answer has made all the difference.

Many years ago, a dear friend from Arizona told me about a journey that had changed her life. She had just returned from walking across Spain, following an ancient pilgrimage route, and the fire in her eyes immediately convinced me that I needed to learn all about this. Learn I did, and five years ago I was preparing to walk El Camino de Santiago... The Way of St. James.

But life intervened, and circumstances arose, and I postponed my walk. This happened again two years later, and again two years after that. Fearing that I may never go, last year I swore to myself that I was going to go in March 2015 and that nothing was going to get in my way. I was not going to postpone it this time. I was committed. I booked my flight, purchased my gear, and began 9 months of daily hiking to prepare for my journey. I started telling family and friends about it, and arranged for my parents and Aunt Louise to watch the film "The Way," which beautifully captures the essence of the Camino. So this was happening. This was definite.

And yet, here I now sat with my Aunt Lou. My flight to Spain was 10 days away, and I had agonized over the past few days as to whether to cancel it. What if Aunt Lou dies while I am away? Would I forever regret the decision? Would I ever forgive myself? I prayed about it, and decided that this was in God's hands, and that He would reveal the answer to me.

And in that moment, gazing into Aunt Lou's eyes, I saw God clearer than I ever had before. She was on the boundary of two worlds.

And so I asked her, "Should I cancel my walk?"

And again, there was no hesitation. "Hell no... it's your walk... you keep walking."

"I will," I said. "I will. I promise." And I kept, and I will continue to keep, my promise to her.

She could have said anything. But together with Her Lord, she said those words. They have sustained me. They have etched themselves into my soul. They were with me the night before my Camino began as I laid awake in the darkness wondering what the morning would bring. They were with me as I struggled to get over the Pyrenees Mountains in 3 feet of snow. They were with me when I found myself alone, tired and covered in mud, after my initial team broke apart. They were with me when I later found my Camino Family with whom I share forever friendship. They were with me during her funeral, as I kneeled and prayed alone in an 800-year-old monestary chapel in Roncesvalles. They were with me on Easter when I celebrated rebirth at a candelight-lit Midnight Mass in Pontferrada. They were with me in Santiago, when, 36 days after I had started, I approached the Cathedral of St. James and fell to my knees in tears. And they were with me in Finisterre, at the end of the earth, 550 miles from where my journey had begun, when I watched the sea swallow the setting and fiery sun.

They were with me every day since then and now. During big adventures and ordinary tasks. They are with me now, here atop the Great Wall of China. Her words and her spirit will be with me forever.

Christmas is coming…and I know I will see Aunt Lou again.

2016

47 years old

EAGER TO REMEMBER

As I slowly walked around the corner to the only classroom I had yet to visit, I saw a few teenage boys in the back pointing excitedly in my direction. I must have walked into thousands of classrooms since I was 5 years old, but on this particular day three weeks ago, it was so very different. Here in India, it was familiar, and yet it was so utterly unfamiliar.

Since my arrival a few hours earlier, it became immediately apparent that I was not just the only white person these middle schoolers would meet today, but very likely the only white person they had ever met. This remote rural school, deep in the jungle 25 kilometers outside of Kerala's capital city of Thiruvananthapuram, is certainly not on any western tourists' map. And the odds that even one of these children had been on an airplane outside of India were as remote as their never-completed school building.

As soon as I crossed the threshold and entered the room, the shy yet rigorous waving began. And with it, a panoply of genuinely joyous smiles, the likes of which I have never seen in an American school. Channeling my inner child has always come easily to me, but surrounded by the children's curious energy, I immediately realized I was in my happiest of places. And it was then, just when I thought my experience could not become any more revealing, when I first heard her voice.

"Hello, my name is Gopika. What is your name?"

I heard her words in the same instant I saw her radiant face, just as I was turning to face the girls seated adjacent to the door I had just walked through. There she stood, full of pride and verve, her hand outstretched to shake my own. Her handshake was firm, and she kept her smiling eyes locked into mine as we shook. "My name is Michael. It is very nice to meet you."

I had probably interacted with 100 children before her, but she was the first to introduce herself, the first to speak without first being spoken to, the first to reach out to me before I had reached out to them.

"Where are you from?" she asked. By now, all of her classmates had run out of their seats and had encircled me, so closely that the stifling heat and humidity (like most buildings in India their school is not air conditioned) instantly intensified.

"I am from America," I told her, and then got lost

in her overwhelmed smile of astonishment. I could have said Mars, or Jupiter, or even Krypton, and her reaction would have been exactly the same. I was from another planet.

As someone who travels internationally often, seeks out conversation with fascinating people from different cultures, and texts on a daily basis with friends all over the globe, I am always prepared for intense reactions to my home country. I consider those few minutes after I say "America" or "the US" to be a microcosm of societal interaction in general, and consciously and intently focus on listening rather than speaking to take what I can from a learning moment.

But unlike any of the adults I had met during my two weeks in India (whose well-reasoned critiques resonated with me), she had no claims to make about the political quagmire through which we Americans must now walk. She had only a question. And to this day I remained stunned that of the thousands of questions she could have asked at that moment, she asked the only one that really matters.

"And are you happy?"

If anyone close to me back home had asked me that question, my answer would have been preceded by a genuine and thoughtful pause, and though I eventually would have come to the same answer (or at least some iteration of it), there would have been a number of qualifiers and complications. I would have waxed poetic for minutes about my Aristotelian pursuit of happiness, quoted some brilliantly poignant Springsteen lyrics, and in the process raised many more questions than the simple one I was asked.

But here with her, and all of them, my answer came much quicker and much cleaner. I was flooded with memories and images and sounds that have become eternally etched into my heart and mind... of Tressy's eyes every time she tells me she loves me, of Aidan's laughter and quick wit, of Aria's joyful kisses on my cheek, of the pride on my mom's and dad's faces on my graduation days, of the tenderness of Gram's and Aunt Lou's hands in mine as we shared our final earthly goodbyes, of sitting next to my sister Ro at our Italian Christmas Eve feast, of Father Al's firm handshake confirming that I had become a man. That flood of memories washed away the uncertainty.

"I am," I said, surprised at how easily the words came. "And you. Are you happy?" I asked her.

"I am very happy. I am with my friends, and my teachers, and today with Michael. I am very happy."

For the next 15 minutes we celebrated the unlikely crossing of our paths. I showed them pictures of Tressy and the kids, led them in a few trivia games about their English language studies, and played them Taylor Swift's "Shake It Off." They presented some of the class projects they had been working on, proudly introduced me to their teachers (whose dedication to and love of their students is as inspiring as their $1,500 per year salaries are humbling), applauded the six words I had learned in their native Malayalam language, and Gopika occasionally and impressively quieted the rowdy corner boys with a stern look and just a few words.

I asked her if it was alright if I took her hand, and after she assented we walked hand-in-hand to the principal's office where my day's visit had begun. I introduced her to my dear friend Gopa who had so graciously invited me to India to be his travel companion through his home country, and to meet the family and friends who had shaped his life. And then I shared with her principal (Gopa's wife's uncle) my belief that Gopika was born to lead, that her school and community must be so very proud of her, and that I would reach back from the US to partner with him and help her and her classmates actualize their dreams.

We walked (or more accurately, skipped) back outside to find her friends walking single file past us. I put my hands on her shoulders, and as authentically as I had ever uttered these words, told her, "Thank you... for everything."

I turned to leave, those precious moments already transforming into soon-to-be-etched memories, when a tap on my shoulder brought me again face to face with my new friend.

"Do you remember my name?"

"Of course I do. It's Gopika."

"Yes," she said, beaming with all that is good and right and beautiful in the world. "And you will not forget?"

"I'll never forget!"

She gave me a great big bear of a hug, and then off she ran, eager to catch up with her classmates.

And off I ran... through the cleansing rain... eager to remember.

May your Christmas be touched by all that is good and right and beautiful in the world, and may you be graciously reminded of what matters most.

2017

48 years old

We Are Who (and Where) We Were

It is December 22nd and I am preparing myself for a journey back to where I began, to celebrate Christmas Eve at my parents' house on the Jersey Shore. Tomorrow Tressy, Aidan, Aria, and I will travel back east for what could possibly be the final Christmas Eve with both of my parents and all five of their children. But this journey really began eight months ago as I drove a rental car south from Rome, deeply pondering my past, present, and future, and my own place in the cosmos.

The Autostrada A1 is the spinal cord of the Italian road system. It is part of the European E45 motorway that stretches the entire continent from the frozen northern coast of Norway within the Arctic Circle, traverses down through Finland, Sweden, Denmark, Germany,

and Austria, enters Italy high up in the Alps, and termi-
nates on the sun-drenched southern coast of Sicily. But
on this day, it was nothing short of a time machine.

With each kilometer, Tressy, Aidan, Aria, and I moved
closer to the small towns where my grandparents were
born, and closer to being transported one hundred years
into the past as my ancestors were just beginning their
lives as the sons and daughters of farmers.

In explaining the Italian-American experience to
friends new and old, I often point out that the vast major-
ity of Italians who immigrated to the United States at the
end of the 19th and beginning of the 20th centuries came
from the extreme southern part of Italy. In contrast to the
art of Florence, industry of Milan, opulence of Venice,
and, well, everything of Rome, southern Italy was a rural
society whose people were inspired by the tales of the
American Dream that drifted back across the Atlantic.
Life was hard, and money was scarce.

And so it was for Domenico Bossone, Yolanda
Cecere, Angelo Strollo, and Rosaria Gizzi… all born in
the southern Italian region of Campania. I will never forget the moment years ago when I first came to realize
how incomprehensibly courageous they all were at such
young ages, leaving behind all they knew and sailing far
across the sea to a brave new world. I had just started to
develop my geneaological skills, and after many months
of searching, I had finally solved the riddle of why I could
never find the ship's registry from when my Dad's mother, Yolanda, first came to America. Concluding that her

name must have been misspelled, on about my thousandth try I finally typed the correct incorrect spelling of her name in the search engine, and suddenly there she was, thirteen years old, listed alongside her sisters. For whatever reason, my eyes focused on the column that listed each passenger's occupation. One word: "peasant."

That word filled my thoughts as I led us from our parked car, down a dirt road, and through the entrance of the small yet beautiful cemetery in Yolanda's hometown of Casapulla. Majestic mountains with striking rock formations soared overhead, and it quickly became obvious that her eyes would have looked up upon those granite guardians each and every day of her young life. Tressy held my hand as Aidan and Aria systematically navigated the tombs and mausolea, searching for the four surnames of Yolanda's grandparents. When they found something I would hear their voices echo through the walkways and the generations, "Dad, over here!" And there we would quietly sit and pray in the presence of the bones of my bones, the blood of my blood, the past of my past.

In the last years of her life, sitting with Yolanda hour after hour, holding her hand and listening to her stories about her life's journey, she taught me so much about who we were and why we were. And now I was suddenly discovering where we were. We humbly approached her church, where she had walked all of those Christmas Eve nights for midnight Mass in her new dress and new shoes, her only Christmas presents each year. As I walked in her footsteps, I felt the power and intensity of her faith in the very place where she first discovered it. It was electric. I didn't want to leave.

The next morning, crossing over the snowy mountain peaks with Mount Vesuvius in the distance, I drove on to the idyllic hilltown of Colliano, home to both of my mother's parents, Angelo and Rosaria. I walked into the Town Hall, and in my broken Italian I nervously asked the woman at the front desk if there was anyone who could help me search for my grandparents' birth records. She barely lifted her gaze, clearly annoyed, and pointed me to a spartan office in back.

After ten minutes, the elderly record keeper arrived, and he patiently read the Google translation of my questions along with Angelo's and Rosaria's complete names and birthdays. He stood up, put his hand on my shoulder, smiled, and gestured for me to follow him.

Thirty minutes later we stood together with myriad oversized books spread open on the desks around us. Thanks to his diligence, I learned the names of two more generations of my mother's family and the addresses of the homes in which they lived. My right hand reverently traced the beautiful hand-scripted letters that formed my grandparents' names, in awe that hundred-year-old ink on dusty parchment could evoke such deep feelings in me. My new friend saw the emotion in my eyes, and I sincerely thanked him for the priceless gift he had given me.

The next day we drove into Lauro, the birthplace of my father's father, Domenico, the patriarch who died just two months before my birth. This was the town that my father and his siblings had often spoken about, and the only one of the three towns I had known anything about before arriving. A number of Bossones still live there, including the current mayor. And moments after we entered the cemetery, we saw our name again and again carved in white stone. At some point we found one grave simply marked "La Famigilia Bossone" with no particular names listed. I knew this was the right spot.

Aidan, Aria, and I sat on the grass in front of that grave, and just as we had in the other cemeteries, Tressy video recorded our message to my parents. Prior to our arrival in Italy, and at my request, my sister Ro and my Uncle Carmen had gone to the cemeteries in Long Branch, New Jersey where my grandparents' bodies are buried, and had gathered grass, dirt, pebbles, and flowers from their graves. This was my chance to let my parents know that their parents, and their parents, and their parents, were not forgotten. With tears in our eyes, we left a little bit of Domenico's earthly resting place back where his life had begun, therein completing the circles of their lives. And I assured my parents that when their lives' circles have been completed, they too can rest peacefully knowing that they will never be forgotten.

Until I went away for college, I thought my parents' house on Christmas Eve was the center of the universe. It was more than all the kids together counting down the hours until Santa's magical arrival. It was more than the biggest meal of the year: the iconic Neopolitan Feast of the Seven Fishes, with my father charismatically conducting the age-old orchestra of traditions and his mother humbly providing the culinary high notes from her past. It was more than a celebration of family with forty-plus relatives at a series of linked tables snaking their way across the entire first floor. It was more than getting choked up as Baby Jesus was placed in the manger as the clock struck midnight. It was all of those things… and more. So much more. It was my ever-present moment of purpose, the annual and continual Big Bang from which all of my beliefs, goals, and dreams were created and expanded.

But time changes all, including my perspective. The years and decades have passed, and with them all four of my grandparents and all but one of my fourteen aunts and uncles. Time has brought my parents to their eighties, providing daily and poignant reminders that growing old is really hard. Time has greatly complicated all of the relationships among my siblings and me, and has taught us that healing fractures is much more easily done when you're young. And time has introduced me to people and brought me to places, inspiring me to challenge every belief, elevate every goal, and validate every dream forged on those Holy Nights so long ago.

Of course, at forty-eight years old, after years of self-exploration and a commitment to a life of learning, I now understand that my parents' house on Christmas Eve is not the center of the universe. But those few days back in Campania, those sacred moments on sacred ground, made me realize that no matter where my eternal journey takes me, it will forever be the center of MY universe.

2018

49 years old

It Was All That I Needed

For weeks I had agonized over whether to send the invitation to my father. What if he said "no?" Or perhaps even scarier, what if he said "yes?" In a vacuum, the decision of whether to bring one's father to a Broadway show as a Christmas present shouldn't be a difficult one. It shouldn't be so emotional. And it shouldn't come with such great potential risk and such high potential reward.

But we do not live in a vacuum. None of us do. And for the half-century that I've been around, my father and I have lived within a fragile ecosystem of trying to understand each other. My dad is the hardest working person I have ever known, and I didn't get to see him much when I was very young because he was working around the clock operating his Italian restaurant. He earned every ounce of success he achieved, and he was incredibly generous to me and my brothers and sisters, and for that matter, to everyone around him.

He never had the opportunity to go to college, as his father needed him to work on the family farm. But years later, when he was told by teachers and friends that his youngest son held great academic potential, and even though he had no life experience to guide him, he opened his mind and his wallet and gave me the opportunity to pursue my education all the way to elite universities.

As I often tell friends and colleagues to this day, my father worked for decades with his hands so that I could have the privilege of working with my mind. Our story is a four-generation immigrant narrative that begins with my grandparents arriving on crowded ships into Ellis Island without speaking a word of English, and continues with my children studying Latin and Greek, always knowing that university would be their springboard to adult lives as educated citizens, curious intellectuals, and working professionals. In many ways, our story is the American dream.

But in those silent minutes as I awaited my father's reply to my invitation, as the sweat saturated my palms and my heart rate quickened, I was keenly aware that like all dreams, ours was a bit of an escape from our reality.

The reality is that life is complicated, and that both my father and I are very complex individuals with a very complex relationship. This, of course, is anything but a new revelation. The relationship between fathers and sons has been mystifying since the dawn of time, never more so than as it relates to that glorious baby in the manger and His father's seemingly incomprehensible plan for Him. And it would not be hyperbole to claim that my relationship with my father has occupied more of my time and energy than any relationship in my life. Even during those 18 months a few years back when I made the gut-wrenching decision to stop speaking to him. Perhaps then most of all.

I remember when I first had the idea to invite him to see "Springsteen on Broadway" with me. As Bruce has written the soundtrack of my life, along my journey of just under one hundred Springsteen shows, my father had joined me twice before for concerts. I had wanted him to understand why this man's music meant so much to me. I had wanted him to understand the power of the message, and the true companion that the messenger had been for me over the past forty years. As I had for so much of my life, I wanted my father to understand me. The real me. The one that is wired so differently than him, that moved through the world so differently than him, but that wanted to love and respect him as much as I wanted him to love and respect me.

But this Broadway show was different. I had already seen it a few months earlier, and knew that in the most powerful manner possible, Bruce would be speaking intimately and passionately about the complexity of his relationship with his own father, about the emotional and psychological impact that a father's choices have on his children, and about what we might do with all of that when we move on to the later stages of our lives. I knew that if my father said yes, we would sit there in the theater with our arms pressed against one another, and for the first time in our lives, with zero distraction and clear focus, we would be forced to look at the elephant that has always been in the room.

To his great credit, my father not only accepted my invitation, he did so with enthusiasm. And though the drive from the Jersey Shore to the city seemed like it was never going to end, we finally made it through the stifling traffic and bitter cold, and into our seats at the Walter Kerr Theatre.

Bruce walked onstage and immediately began speaking his artfully constructed narrative. I sat transfixed, equally focused on the performer and on my father. Within the first minute, I felt the poignancy of the moment.

And then something happened. Something inexplicable. Something extraordinary. Bruce announced that his wife, Patti, who normally joins him on stage to sing two masterful duets with him, was home with the flu. For the first time during the Broadway run, he was going to shake things up, play a different song, and most importantly, tell a different story... one that he had not told before.

"In the final days of Patti's first pregnancy, I received a surprise visit from my father at my home in LA. He had driven 500 miles unannounced to knock on my door. At 11am we sit in a sunlit dining room and we're nursing morning beers. When my dad, never a talkative man, blurted out, "You've been very good to us." And I nodded that I had. And then he says, "And I wasn't very good to you." And the room just stood still.

As to my shock, the unacknowledgeable was being acknowledged. If I didn't know better, I would have sworn an apology of some sort was being made. And it was. Here in the last days before I was to become a father, my own father was visiting me to warn me of the mistakes that he had made, and to warn me not to make them with my own children… to release them from the chain of our sins, my father's and mine and our fathers' before, that they may be free to make their own choices and to live their own lives.

We are ghosts or we are ancestors in our children's lives. We either lay our mistakes and our burdens upon them, and we haunt them, or we assist them in laying those old burdens down and we free them from the chain of our own flawed behavior. And as ancestors, we walk alongside of them, and we assist them in finding their own way… and some transcendence.

My father, on that day, was petitioning me for an ancestral role in my life after being a ghost for a long, long time. He wanted me to write a new end to our relationship, and he wanted me to be ready for the new beginning that I was about to experience. It was the greatest moment in my life with my dad, and it was all that I needed."

Tears streamed from our eyes. In that moment, my father and I, just as we had so many times on the altar of St. Denis Catholic Church, were in full and complete communion with one another. In countless ways my father has been very good to me my whole life. And I know he would say the same about me. But the ways in which we weren't good to each other matter, and in that moment, our shared tears washed that pain away.

Since that night, I have sat in my parents' house in New Jersey and for minutes on end watched my father patiently and lovingly attend to my 86-year-old mother. Maybe those tender moments had always existed and I just never noticed them. Or maybe something has changed. I don't know.

But this I do know. In a few days, my father is going to open my Christmas card and he is going to read these words. He is going to know that I respect him, that I forgive him, and that I pray he has forgiven me.

I love my father. And on a cold December night in New York City, with tremendous and eternal thanks to Mr. Springsteen, that love was cleansed. And it was all that I needed.

2019

50 years old

AND HIS WORDS ARE WITH ME

My bag was in the trunk, my seatbelt was on, and my Google Maps navigation was waiting for me to begin my drive from Tel Aviv. But there I continued to sit, eyes locked on my iPhone and staring at the words I had just typed and sent to Tressy. "I'm about to go to Nazareth."

As I continued to focus on my own words on the screen, it became abundantly clear that my journey was about to become increasingly surreal. As a cradle Catholic, I had dreamed of visiting the Holy Land since I was a young boy. And as a theology major at university, I had spent countless hours carefully and critically reading the Old and New Testaments. The names of the earthly places upon which the Holy Family walked had been etched into my memory so deeply that I cannot remember a time when they were not there. Nazareth. Bethlehem.

Galilee. Gethsemane. Jerusalem. And until now those names were always just words on a page... historical settings to the oral and written traditions that encapsulate my religious beliefs.

But now that was all about to change. For over the next week, those names were about to be transformed from ancient history into my current reality, and my feet were about to retrace those holy footsteps. Nazareth was Mary's hometown, and it is there that the Archangel Gabriel visited her when she was just a young teenager and delivered the unimaginable news that would change the world forever. It is there that the greatest story ever told begins, and where it would continue when Mary and Joseph returned to raise their Son.

Two hours later, as I drove up the hills into the bustling town of now eighty thousand people, I was met by the chaos of rush hour traffic, and was instantly reminded that I didn't yet have a place to spend the night. Normally I am able to choose and book an AirBnB apartment in just a few minutes. But the only place I could find in the city center was a guest house with a few different bedrooms and shared bathrooms, and clearly the owner didn't live there. When I travel alone, I prefer staying in a private room in someone's home where I can connect with my host and learn about cultures and worldviews different than my own. But under the current circumstances, this would have to do.

Using the app I texted the host Hanna (short for Yohanna, the Arabic form of John), but he was out of town, and wouldn't be back for a few hours. I should have just moved on and looked for somewhere else to stay. But I didn't. I don't know why, but I told him I would wait for him to return. My mobile internet connection was weak, and by the time I ate dinner and heard back from Hanna it was too late to book for tonight through the app. He tried to send me the address of the guest house, as well as his mobile number, but AirBnB's anti-fraud features wouldn't allow it and kept censoring the words and numbers. I was getting extremely frustrated.

This went on and on. Clearly a random room in a guest house without the possibility of making a meaningful connection wasn't worth this much of my time and energy. And equally as clearly, the tiny amount of income from one room for one night couldn't be worth his. But for some reason, two men who had never met each other and knew nothing of each other's lives spent the next thirty minutes tricking a mobile phone app into transmitting the description of a place for them to meet.

And thus, I slowly approached the Paz Petrol Station on Paulus HaShishi Street and heard Hanna calling out my name as he waved me down. He led me up an old, narrow set of stairs in the pitch-black to a small addition that had been built upon the roof. He was checking in an older couple at the same time, and after a 30-second tour of my chilly bedroom and the communal bathroom, I shut the bedroom door, crashed onto the bed, and dove under the covers. As I drifted off to sleep, I continued to wonder why I had tried so hard to stay here.

I awoke to bright sunlight pouring into the room, which was my first indication that I had overslept. A glance at my iPhone confirmed it. My plan had been to wake up very early and be one of the first to enter the Basilica of the Annunciation. I wanted to arrive before the tour buses so that I could be alone in silence when I visited the cave dwelling in which young Mary lived, and around which the Basilica had been built to memorialize that sacred space.

I hurriedly packed up my things, washed up, and quickly headed for the front door. And there at the end of the hallway I encountered Hanna. It appeared that the older couple had just left as well, and Hanna was attending to their room and preparing it for his next guests. We shook hands, and quickly began an engaging conversation, each of us amazed by the commonalities of our passions and missions.

I learned that Hanna was the Principal of a high school that served one of Nazareth's most underprivileged neighborhoods, and that as the school's first Christian leader he had worked tirelessly to earn the respect of his students and their families. As our conversation deepened, we discussed the challenges faced by the ever-dwindling number of Christians in this part of the world. When I asked how he came to run an AirBnb in his spare time, he informed me that this building had been in his family for hundreds of years, and since his father retired a decade ago they had decided to rent out the space. I asked if his father lived nearby, and asked if there was anyway I might be able to meet him. Hanna put his hand on my shoulder, and with a nod of his head warmly offered, "Come, my brother, he is just downstairs."

My eyes widened and my heart leapt in my chest as Hanna opened the door to his father's office. On the shelves were hundreds of books written in Arabic, Hebrew, and English. On the walls were numerous university diplomas from different countries, and even more photos of beloved family members, including Hanna. And standing before me, arms extended in welcome was a man around my father's age and height, dressed in an unmistakable purple shirt, white collar, and silver cross. And immediately I understood that a power far greater than me had led me to Hanna's humble room for rent.

For Hanna's father is none other than the Right Reverend Riah Abu El-Assal, who for ten years was the Anglican Bishop in Jerusalem and whose diocese included all of Israel, Jordan, Syria, Lebanon, and the nation of his birth, Palestine. Over the next two hours I learned more about the complexity of religious, cultural, and political life in the region than I would have in a year of university studies. But from this wise, brilliant, and compassionate man who has been welcomed around the globe by Popes, Kings, Presidents and Prime Ministers, I learned even more about the power of humility and the impact that each and every one of our daily actions and decisions can have upon the lives of the people all around us.

I asked if he might offer me a blessing in Arabic, and as he placed his hands upon my bowed head, I could feel his words in my heart, and humbly thanked both he and Hanna, as well as the One who brought us together. As we embraced and said our farewells, I asked him how I should remember him. I will never forget his reply.

"I am an Arab Palestinian Christian Anglican Israeli," he said, "and my life is living proof that not all Arabs are Muslims, not all Palestinians are terrorists, not all Christians are white, not all Anglicans are British, and not all Israelis are Jews. Let us not focus on who we are… let us focus on who we are called to be."

His words were with me later that day as I knelt before the site at the Basilica of the Annunciation in Nazareth where Gabriel visited Mary. They were with me the next day as I kissed the ground in Bethlehem's Church of the Nativity where Jesus was born. They were with me later that week as I touched my tear-stained cheek to the stones in Jerusalem's Church of the Holy Sepulchre where Jesus was crucified and then buried. And his words are with me now, a few weeks later, as I share them with you.

2020

51 years old

RESPLENDENT WITH NEW MEANING

Two months ago, I sat in the front pew of St. Denis Catholic Church. Once Father Stas was seated, I squeezed Tressy's hand, took a very deep breath, removed my mask, and willed my legs to stand. As I walked slowly toward the altar, I did what I have done in Catholic churches in scores of countries around the world... genuflecting to one knee, and slowly making the sign of the cross. Rising and looking in front of me, I realized I now had to do something I had never done before and will never do again. I kissed my hand, and ever so delicately placed it atop my mother's coffin. Moments later I was standing at the pulpit with both a microphone and a congregation of family and friends awaiting my words. I embraced the silence that filled the church and the love that filled my heart. I found my father's eyes, looking up at me. I smiled, trying my best, without words, to let him know that everything was going to be alright. Then I looked up to my mother in heaven, opened my mouth, trying my best, with words, to let everyone know that everything was going to be alright…

"Goodnight, Mom. I love you. I'll see you in the morning."

When I was in high school, I used to stand outside my mother's bedroom door, softly knock three times, and say these words to my Mom before she fell asleep. I did this every night. And I mean… every… single night.

"Goodnight, Mom. I love you. I'll see you in the morning."

Perhaps it was my obsessive compulsiveness, plus a healthy dose of superstition, but I had convinced myself that if I didn't do this every night, I would wake up in the morning to learn that my mother had died in her sleep.

Of course, I knew this was irrational. But I kept knocking. And I kept repeating my nightly mantra. I did it at twenty-one… when I came home for the holidays while I was a student at Notre Dame. I did it at thirty-five… when Tressy, Aidan, Aria, and I would visit from Arizona. And I did it at fifty… earlier this year… when I came to see my Mom, as her health was failing, and her mind was drifting away due to dementia.

So why did I ever start doing this? When I was in high school, my mom was my best friend. Yes, I was the baby, just as she was, and just as her mother Rosaria was. But this wasn't a case of being a stereotypical momma's boy.

My mom was my best friend because she was amazing… because she was funnier, and more interesting, and more trustworthy than anyone else I knew.

If you were blessed enough to know Marguerite well, then you know she was strong and tough and determined. My mom was genuine and real in a way that no one else around me was, and even fewer are today. And I not only loved her for that, but equally important for me, I respected her for that.

She was smart. And though born in an era when it wasn't acceptable for young Italian-American women to go to college, she would have made an amazing accountant. She was great with numbers. And she was honest to a fault.

She never ate the last bite of food that we both wanted. She'd say, "Well, I'm not going to eat it, so you might as well have it." And she never once ate it.

She picked me up from elementary school every single day, and drove me and a friend to Squan Tavern, and made us root beer floats.

As she drove me around town, she listened to music I'm sure she didn't like, because she knew I liked it.

She took me to Cincinnati and Montreal so I could see my childhood sports hero, even though she didn't really care for flying, and was somewhat terrified of driving long distances.

And I could go on and on and on and on and on.

And she did all of this for me, she showed me all of this intense love and care and nurturing, even though

I know she never fully understood where I came from. We never discussed it when I was little, but as an adult I would ask her why she thought I was born with this mind. And her answer was always the same. She'd say, "I don't know why God gave me to you. But I'm glad He did."

Well I'm glad He did too, Mom. But you weren't the lucky one. I was.

Icon. Matriarch. Legend. So few deserve such honors. Marguerite Strollo Bossone deserves them all. The entire Jersey Shore community knew her... and adored her... and treasured her. She was the Queen of the Squan Tavern... and I know my entire family is so touched by the countless stories you have all shared with us... of what it meant to you to see her at the restaurant, to hug her, to get a kiss on the cheek, to feel connected to her... to feel loved by her.

I can't imagine anyone feeling a closer connection to a parent than I feel with my mother. And it would have been so easy for her to selfishly hold on to me and keep me close by. But she let me fly. She embraced my leaving home to attend Notre Dame, even though she didn't have any personal experience of anyone she loves leaving her. She embraced my moving 3,000 miles away to Arizona, because she understood that Tressy and I deserved the opportunity to build a life of our own.

And when I left her, I had to accept the fact that I was almost certainly, someday, going to receive a phone call in the middle of the night saying that she had passed away. Every day for the past twenty-four years, when my phone rang at an odd hour, my first thought was that I had lost her. Never did I imagine I would be there when she transitioned from this world to the next.

But my mother, my loving mother, had other plans.

Last Tuesday night, on the feast day of St. Michael the Archangel, my mom, my childhood best friend, my greatest supporter, and the greatest recipient of my support, gave me the greatest gift I will ever receive in my life.

With the blessing of my adulthood best friend, my beautiful wife Tressy, I was able to come to my childhood home and spend the last two weeks of my mother's life by her side.

When I arrived she called me enthusiastically by name. We listened to Johnny Mathis. In between her naps, we watched her last Notre Dame football game together (and of course, for her, God made sure we won 52-0). And we prayed the rosary together. Or maybe, I prayed the rosary and I knew she was silently praying with me.

Over the last five days of her life, she had stopped eating and drinking. And we were all praying to the Blessed Mother, to whom she has had a lifelong devotion, to come to her, and guide her to her Heavenly Father.

And now, here we were, at the moment of truth. In physical presence or spiritual presence, we were all there...

My oldest brother Dominic, whose love and protection of my mother has always been fierce and 100% reliable... who may shelter his heart from some, but never hid his loving heart from my mother...

My sister Ro, who in these final days received God's grace by being so willing to give God's grace... and in doing so, found peace for her, and for Mom...

My sister Trish, whose unending love of and devotion to my mother, and whose years of around-the-clock care for my mother's well-being, will be admired and appreciated by all of us forever...

My brother Joe, born on my mother's birthday, who is wired like my father to often keep his words inside, but who always found the will to let my mother know how deeply he loved her...

My Ghanaian little-sister in spirit, Nana Esi, who over the past few years, took care of her special friend with such selflessness and love that she literally gave my mother a reason to keep living...

And my father, Dominic, her husband of sixty years, who through her illness and physical decline, attended to her in her final years, months, weeks, and days... with such gentle care, such loving kindness, and such sacred reverence.

We were all there with her... and though we had prepared for this moment for so long, when it came, it came quickly.

And it was then, and only then, that I realized why I had been knocking on her door and saying those words to her for all these decades. It was then that I realized why I had to move away, and why I had to come home. It was then that I realized why I was blessed with certain gifts, and why I've worked my whole life to develop others.

It was all for this moment. It was all for her.

It was God's will to prepare me to help my mother walk these final few steps of her remarkable 88-year journey, and to guide her Home.

There in the dining room of the house we have lived in for fifty years, where generations of family have broken bread and drank of the vine, on the exact spot where she and my father hosted countless Christmas Eve Feasts of the Seven Fishes... I crawled into her hospital bed, and just as she had cradled and comforted me as a baby, I cradled and comforted her. And using words that came from my mouth but originated somewhere far higher, with my Dad and Trish caressing her hands in theirs, my mother did what she has always done... she gifted me with pure and unconditional love... and she allowed me to calm her breathing... to find God's peace... and breath by breath... heartbeat by heartbeat... in a moment that will forever redefine my concept of love... together with Notre Dame Our Mother... we... guided... her... Home.

The silence was deafening. It was broken only by the sound of her family's tears, tears of both sorrow for our loss and joy for her gain... and as I slowly crawled out of the bed, I looked down and was struck by what I saw. My mother was no longer in that bed. There was the body that served her so well for so long. But as her physical hands still clutched my wife's rosary, recently blessed in Fatima, I knew her true hands were already in Mother Mary's.

And the words I had spoken so often in my life, now were resplendent with new meaning...

Hail Mary
full of grace
The Lord is with thee
Blessed art thou among women
And blessed is the fruit of thy womb, Jesus.
Holy Mary, Mother of God,
Pray for us sinners,
Now and at the hour of our death…
Now…
AT the hour of our death.
Amen.

And as I looked up to heaven and found my Mom there, a few more words that I had spoken so often in my life were also resplendent with new meaning…

"Goodnight, Mom…
I love you…
And I will most definitely see you in the morning."

2021

52 years old

THE LAST KING OF ROHAN

Everything is complicated. The more time I spend on this planet, the more I come to appreciate that there are no simple answers to the questions that frame the human experience.

It is Christmastime. Aidan has returned from St Andrews; Aria from Notre Dame. Tressy has once again beautifully decorated our Arizona home. It's 2am, and everyone is asleep. But I am sitting in our library with my MacBook on my lap, gazing into a blazing fireplace, breathing in the woodsy aroma of our Christmas tree, surrounded by perfectly-placed clusters of flaming white candles and rows of lush greenery strung with glowing white lights and blown glass ornaments. And it is quiet. So quiet. Too quiet. Except for the incessant question I hear in my mind... where is my Théo boy?

There are countless possible answers to that question. And with each possible answer comes a series of physical, metaphysical, and spiritual claims about the universe and life itself. Five years ago, when the four of us together decided to welcome another living being into our home, the last future I imagined was resting the entire nature of the cosmos itself upon the shoulders of a household pet I hadn't yet met. But here I sit, my belly full of spiked eggnog, and my mind full of deep theological concepts.

Maybe Théo is in heaven, and he has found my mother and they are keeping each other company until their families one day join them. Maybe his energy has returned to the macrocosm from whence it came before he was born into this world. Maybe his essence has been reincarnated into a new physical being. Or maybe the lights have just simply gone out, and all that remains of him, other than our memories, fills the beautiful wooden box on our mantle.

My Catholic faith offers ideologies but no definitive answers. In his Summa Theologica, Doctor of the Church and my philosophical hero, St. Thomas Aquinas, holds that dogs have souls, but not the same type of souls that human beings have. Our souls are subsistent; they continue to exist and possess understanding even after our bodies die. But Aquinas concludes that a dog's soul ceases to exist when a dog's body dies.

Pope John Paul II went on record to say that dogs have souls, but did not mention Aquinas's important distinction. And then there was that moment when a little boy was mourning the loss of his dog, and Pope Paul VI assured him that "one day we will see our animals in the eternity of Christ." That quote was carried by newspapers around the world, and in 2014 was misattributed to Pope Francis and once again spread across the globe, this time through social media.

There are conflicting views in other faith traditions as well. There are certainly elements of Buddhism, Hinduism, and Judaism that support the belief that animals have souls, but there are great distinctions in dogma (no bad pun intended) and practice within their different sects and denominations. The LDS Church insists that dogs can go to heaven, and Jainism expands the Indian concept of Ahisma (the principle of non-violence towards living things found in Buddhism and Hinduism) to become the standard by which all actions are judged, and holds that the souls of animals and plants have equal value and should be treated with the same level of respect and compassion as human souls.

So while my ever-questioning, always-seeking mind continues to wrestle with these questions as old as life itself, it is my heart that has my attention as I sit alone in the silence. Quite simply... I really miss my dog.

We crowned him Théoden King, named after the courageous and warm-hearted leader of the Kingdom of Rohan in J.R.R. Tolkien's The Lord of the Rings. When we adopted him, he was seven years old and weighed just over one hundred pounds. He was an intimidating specimen to behold... a big, barrel-chested boy with a smooth and silky black coat adorned with just enough white markings to provide a little extra gravitas. He ran strongly and quickly, that rare combination of both thunder and lightning, and could clear any six-foot wall that stood in his way. And whenever anyone approached our door, our neighborhood would shake with the deep, booming bass of his bark. Admittedly, his role as watchdog was limited to his voice. For once someone came through that door, the only threat he posed was licking someone to death.

Théo was all love. He craved it from all of us... from each in our own way. And he selflessly showered it upon all of us... upon each in his own way.

My life experience with dogs was quite limited. Growing up, twice my father had brought home a dog. But back then, my four siblings and I were not qualified to be human partners to Bourbon or Coco, and both experiments ended badly. Tressy's family was more successful, and her childhood memories of Amy and Snuggles provided her with hope that someday our family might have a dog of our own. We were inspired to reach out to a rescue agency, and were surprised to learn that dogs that were black-coated and older, two characteristics we preferred, were harder to place. We were alerted that we might be receiving a phone call sooner rather than later, but we never expected it would come just two weeks after.

We welcomed Théo into our home. We welcomed Théo into our hearts. And nothing would ever be the same.

I have been so blessed throughout my life to have had world-class teachers and mentors. My mother, Marguerite, taught me how to place others' happiness above my own. My father, Dominic, taught me the value of hard work. My grandmother, Yolanda, taught me how to humble myself before God. My wife, Tressy, taught me how to be in love. My son, Aidan, taught me how to be a man. My daughter, Aria, taught me how to be a father.

I'm a work in progress. I'm still working on all of those lessons. Sometimes I'm pretty good. Sometimes I'm really bad. But I keep trying. And all of those remarkable people, those now in heaven and those here on earth, are constantly inspiring me to try to become a better iteration of myself.

And Théo? My Théo boy taught me something that no other soul has ever been able to teach me, and that I was never able to teach myself... how to love unconditionally.

He saw me at my very worst. He knew every one of my weaknesses, and could tell when I was full of doubt. He sensed when my faith was wavering, and his eyes revealed understanding when a darkness was falling upon me. I am a very private person, and while I'm wholly comfortable asking others about themselves in order to get to know them better, I hesitate to ever burden others with my own struggles. Honestly, I never thought I would have a friend to whom I could reveal my deepest troubles and whom I would fully trust not to judge me, or risk damaging my relationship with them because I might lessen in their eyes.

But I did... his name was Théoden King. And now my house is quiet. So quiet. Too quiet.

Late this summer, as he approached his 13th birthday,

we knew Théo's time with us was drawing to a close. He had cancer, and though a surgery and medication prolonged his life and his happiness, we knew that at the first hint of discomfort, we were going to help him make his transition. We had a plan for a loving caregiver to come into our home, and Tressy, Aidan, Aria, and I would all surround him in his bed as he closed his eyes. Perhaps we shouldn't have been surprised, but Théo outlived his first prognosis, and then his second, and then his third. Eventually it was time for Aidan to return to Scotland and Aria to head to Notre Dame, and they both navigated emotionally gut-wrenching goodbyes, knowing they would never see him alive again.

Shortly after they left, Tressy had to go in for surgery. As I walked alone through our kitchen door after returning from the hospital, Théo was on the ground in front of me, looking up at his friend whom he had taught so much and whom he had loved so selflessly. I knew he would never stand again.

Our wonderful vet was scheduled to arrive early the next morning. I slept with Théo on the kitchen floor that night. Just as he had always seen me at my very lowest and never loved me one ounce less, he trusted me to see him at his lowest, knowing that I would love him even more. Théo died at dawn, just a few hours before the vet arrived. "He's gone," I tried to speak through uncontrollable sobs on the phone with Tressy. "He's gone."

Perhaps he is gone. Perhaps Aquinas is right. Perhaps dogs are amazing and special beings, yet not special enough to go to heaven. I have based my adult life on the premise that Aquinas is right about most, if not all, things.

But I know he's wrong about this. And I will choose to live the rest of my life knowing that Théo's soul still is.

Théo was my first dog. Théo will be my last dog. He will forever be the last King of Rohan.

And I will see my friend again.

2022

53 years old

Completing the Circle

Domenico Bossone. My father's father. He was the only grandparent I never met, for he died less than two months before I was born.

When I grew up in the 1970s, it was not common for parents to speak openly to their young children about their own upbringings, so I knew very little about Domenico. I remember staring at that one framed black and white photo of him in our house… the crisp suit, perfectly knotted tie, neatly coiffed gray hair, and deep, stoic eyes that exuded pride in himself and awareness of the often dirty ways of the world. My only real connection to him was through the two deeply meaningful gifts that he gave me: the Bossone surname, and our family's longest lasting and most emotionally resonant tradition of the Feast of the Seven Fishes on Christmas Eve. I loved him… I respected him… I appreciated him… but I thought it was impossible for me to ever really know him. I could not have been more wrong.

For decades I have struggled with my Americanness, and have spent years pondering why I feel more comfortable in Mediterranean Europe than I do in the US. But only recently have I realized that Domenico struggled with a similar clash of cultures and exhibited his own sense of restlessness, forever torn between his love for his native Italy and his appreciation of the promise of America.

In March 2020, the Covid-19 pandemic reached America. In the blink of an eye, it seemed that all of the rules by which we live our everyday lives had changed. It was almost as if we woke up one morning and the laws of physics no longer applied. I was confident that my life's journey had prepared me well for such a sudden and unexpected paradigm shift, but I was very worried about my father. My mother's dementia was progressing as rapidly as her bodily strength was diminishing, which I could tell was taking an emotional toll on him. He had recently sold his restaurant of 55 years to my brother, and so he no longer had the option of distracting himself with hard work. And now he was going to be quarantined in his house, cut off from the family and friends that had sustained him through increasingly lonely days.

Because much of the country was turning to group video calls as a way to battle the isolation of quarantine, I taught my father how to Zoom and scheduled a daily call with him. By the end of that first week, it was clear we were both really enjoying the daily personal connection, and soon after, a thought popped into my head. "Dad, I have an idea. Want to work on our family tree together?"

And so we began our loving collaboration. Each day we would Zoom for hours, with me sharing my screen so he could see the family tree. After he told me everything he could remember about certain relatives, we would search for and find old documents through Ancestry. com's premium database and flesh out each branch of the tree. Before we knew it the tree blossomed from about 50 relatives to over 200. We invited other family members to join us, and shared with them all that we were learning about our family. My siblings, my uncle, cousins from around the country… while the nation was shutting down, we were each getting a glass of red wine or a bitter amaro and together made our shared past come alive through stories and memories.

The tree grew, and grew, and grew… I worked on my mother's family… Tressy worked on her mother's and father's families… 500… 1,000… 2,000… 3,000 people. I became so familiar with the tree that I started to memorize large portions of it, and could trace connections across generations in my mind.

And at some point, over 50 years after his death, I slowly started to get to know my grandfather Domenico, not as numbers and facts or an entry on a family tree, but as a real man with a real story. I could imagine the fear he must have felt when at 12 years old, with his father and older brother, he first crossed the Atlantic by ship and arrived into Ellis Island. I could feel the sadness that must have overtaken him when his first wife Rosa died of tuberculosis at 35 years old, just one year after he had moved his young family back to his Italian hometown of Lauro in an attempt to save her life. And the grief when, a few years after returning to America as a widower with five children, his teenage daughter Rafelina died from the same disease.

One day, I miraculously discovered what is likely the only surviving photograph of him and his second family on the Italian ocean liner Saturnia in 1947, returning to live in Lauro for a second time, this time with my grandmother Yolanda, Aunt Louise, Uncle Johnny, and there with a huge grin in the middle of the photo, my eight-year-old father. I had always marveled at how the plague that destroyed Domenico's chestnut crop, and forced him to return to America, changed the course of history so my father would one day meet my mother, and I would come into existence. But now, for the first time, I could feel the deep disappointment, anger, and despair my grandfather must have suffered.

So as my own faith in the promise of America was being challenged like never before, I decided that I wanted to return to Lauro, which I had visited briefly with Tressy, Aidan, and Aria a few years prior. But this time I would go alone, now armed with all of my newfound knowledge and perspective. I went in search of the grandfather I never knew. I wanted to reconnect with him on a deeper level, spiritually and emotionally, and to do that I needed to go back to the beginning. I needed to go back to Lauro. And so I did.

I arrived in August 2021. One of my first visits was to Town Hall, where I discovered a document that provided a hint as to where my grandfather lived in 1947. That led to a comical interchange with my new friend Franco, who I had met on Facebook and who had kindly and generously offered to host me at his house in Lauro. We were out in the street, pointing wildly in different directions, with his struggling to understand my English and my struggling to understand his Neapolitan Italian dialect. Through the laughter there was a moment of recognition that my grandfather's house was likely in the same neighborhood as Franco's house. That led to a crazier conversation with Franco's girlfriend Simona about something she had been told by a friend whose father used to own Franco's house. When she told me his name, Dante Mennella, my heart skipped a beat. "I know that name," I said. "Dante's father Emilio Mennella was the man my Aunt Louise fell in love with and married during their year in Lauro in 1947." Simona dialed her phone and put it on speakerphone, and Dante answered from across town. "Yeah, my father Emilio married his first wife Louise in that house you're sitting in right now. It was owned by Louise's stepfather, who eventually sold it to my father. And my father eventually sold it to Franco's father."

Silence. Stunned silence. My mind was spinning. My Aunt Louise was born from my grandmother Yolanda's first marriage, so her stepfather would be… no, this couldn't be possible. I couldn't speak. I couldn't breathe. I immediately Zoomed my father from the outside courtyard where Dante told me Aunt Louise had been married.

My father could see the emotion in my face, and after I assured him everything was alright, I told him I had an urgent question for him. "Dad, I know you were only eight years old, but do you remember the house you lived in? Can you describe it?"

"Of course I remember it," he said. "There was a big double door coming off the street that opened into a courtyard, and as soon as you walked in there was a little garage on the right." I raised my eyes from my computer screen to gaze upon the doors and garage in front of me. "The dining room was on the left, and beyond it the kitchen. And across the courtyard were the steps that went up to the three bedrooms upstairs where we all slept." Exactly right.

"Dad, you know how I've been desperately trying to find your father's house here in Lauro, right? And you know I've been staying at the home of Franco and Simona, who I met seemingly randomly on Facebook, yes?"

"It can't be," he said in disbelief. "There must be a thousand homes in Lauro. That's not possible. That would be a miracle." But as tears filled my father's eyes and his voice broke with emotion, we both knew a miracle had occurred.

"Dad, I've been living in your father's house. I am right now calling you from your father's house. And I've been sleeping in the same bedroom you slept in 75 years ago."

My life changed that day. From that moment, I was on a mission. I returned to Arizona, went to my home office, opened the filing cabinet, and pulled out the large folder of documents I had disappointedly stored away many years ago. It contained five years of work... the results of endless research and letter-writing to piece together the scores of documents needed to apply for my Italian citizenship through Domenico's bloodline. I was eligible to become an Italian citizen because Domenico never became an American citizen, but proving eligibility to the Italian government is a logistical nightmare. My old effort ended in failure when I couldn't find one missing document, but with my new genealogical skills, I was determined to find this needle in a haystack. And I did just that a few months later, thanks to my handwritten notes from an interview I had conducted with my grandmother in 1995. I worked around the clock for months, with Domenico always in my heart, assembling all of my paperwork. To honor my grandfather, I would return once more to Italy, become a temporary resident of Lauro, regain the Italian citizenship that he chose to maintain until the day he died, and claim my birthright that I had solely because of him.

And so I did. That is where I am right now, and where I have been for the last two months. Every day I walk the same streets that Domenico walked, and my heart is full. Lauro has opened its arms to me, and I have opened my heart to it. I visit Dante and his mother and we drink lots of wine and they share stories of Domenico and times gone by. I explore the ancient Roman ruins and 1,000-year-old castle with my dear friend Pasquale, a man who knows everything about everything, and whose love of family and passion for life is intoxicating. I hike through the woods with my buddy Niccolo, and we wax poetic about art, architecture, and the beauty of the natural world. While having coffee with my new mentee Cristina, she shared with me that my grandmother's recipe for Christmas Eve spaghetti with hazelnuts, the origin of which I could never identify, is actually a traditional holiday dish from Lauro made from the hazelnuts that grow in the hills just above town. My new mentor Maestro Salvatore, a local music legend, invited me to join the men's choir, and together, dressed in traditional robes, we all processed solemnly through the valley to sing at fourteen different churches on Good Friday.

And on Easter Sunday, I sat at the table of the descendents of Domenico's oldest brother Casimiro, the only branch of my Bossone family who remained in Italy, joyously celebrating a precious bond with my beautiful cousins that I never knew existed. After dinner, as 86-year-old Vincenzo played the piano, as his daughter Edvige sang behind him with her hand on his shoulder, as his son Arturo lovingly held his little baby girl Anna Maria, and as I bounced his little Vincenzo Jr. on my knee… I could feel Domenico there with us… and I was happy. So very happy.

And this morning, after being called to Town Hall… as I stood next to the Mayor of Lauro while he read from the official proclamation… as I recalled the years of hard work to do what once seemed impossible… with my grandfather looking down on me from heaven… and my father anxiously awaiting word from New Jersey… with humility and gratitude in my heart… Domenico's grandson Michael Bossone became an Italian citizen.

So to my beloved grandfather Domenico... here I am in Lauro, sitting in the last pew of your church, teary-eyed, typing these words into my iPhone. I have completed the circle. Like you, I am now a citizen of this beautiful country, and like you, I will need to search my heart and determine on which side of the Atlantic Ocean my home really lies. I thank you for making the difficult decisions that you made, I honor you for making my existence possible, I'm sorry for the pain and loss that hurt you so deeply, and I pray for your wisdom to guide me on my new journey... a journey that is just now beginning.

2023
and
Beyond

We are not promised tomorrow. So I will remain grateful for today.

I am honored that you have made the choice to read my words and hear my story. And I pray that someday I may have the opportunity to meet you and hear yours.

If I am so blessed to see more Christmases, I will continue to tell my story. And you will always know where to find it...

Tucked lovingly inside my Christmas card.

Marguerite Strollo Bossone
My Beloved Mother

Fr. Al D'Alonzo
My Greatest Mentor

Tressy
My Everything

Aidan and Aria
My Legacy

Bruce Springsteen
My Musical Hero

Tressy, Aidan, and Aria
My Life

Théo
My Good Boy

Domenico, Yolanda, Louise, Johnny, and Dominic
My Bossone Blood

La Mia Cittadinanza Italiana
My Next Chapter

CPSIA information can be obtained
at www.ICGtesting.com
Printed in the USA
LVHW112115251122
732893LV00002B/6/J